THE
COMPUTER
NETWORKING
HANDBOOK

By

Trevor Shelwick

Table of Contents

Chapter 1: Basics of Networking

1.1 Defining Networking

Networking essentially connects various digital devices to streamline the flow and exchange of information. This capability extends from modest local networks within a single office to vast global networks linking millions of devices worldwide. The functions of networking are as diverse as its uses, supporting everything from elementary file sharing among individuals to sophisticated, real-time data exchanges crucial for multinational enterprises.

Through networking, devices can interact seamlessly, facilitating numerous tasks such as emailing, video streaming, conducting virtual meetings, and utilizing cloud services. More than just transferring data, networking enables real-time collaboration across different geographic locations. This dynamic interaction of data involves a complex orchestration of data packets that travel through cables, airwaves, and optical fibers, all regulated by meticulously crafted protocols that manage data flow.

Delving deeper, networking combines an understanding of both hardware and software. Network hardware, including routers, switches, and hubs, directs traffic efficiently across the network, while network software involves the operating systems and applications that leverage network capabilities. Protocols ensure seamless communication across devices, irrespective of their specifications or operating systems.

A key component of networking is its topology, which refers to the network's layout. These can range from simple structures, like a star topology where each device connects to a central hub, to more complex arrangements like a mesh topology with devices interconnected in a web-like structure, enhancing the reliability and speed of data transmission.

The evolution of networking technology has notably transitioned from traditional wired connections to more sophisticated wireless solutions, reflecting broader technological advancements and evolving user demands. Modern networks are designed to be highly adaptable, scalable, and secure, supporting extensive device connections while protecting sensitive data against cyber threats.

In essence, networking underpins modern digital communications and is a vital field of study and application in today's tech-driven world. By optimizing network setups, we enhance operational efficiency and foster innovations that reshape our living and working environments. Thus, a well-crafted network is not merely a technological structure but a strategic asset that boosts performance, enhances security, and drives success across various sectors.

1.2 The Evolution of Network Technology

The narrative of network technology's evolution begins in the late 1950s and early 1960s with the advent of the first computers capable of sharing information. This era set the foundation for what would later become the internet, initially comprising basic networks that connected terminals to mainframe computers within confined spaces like buildings or campuses. The transformation deepened with the creation of ARPANET in the late 1960s, a pivotal project funded by the U.S. Department of Defense designed to establish a robust, fault-tolerant, and distributed network.

The introduction of packet switching by ARPANET marked a revolutionary shift, significantly enhancing the efficiency and reliability of communication over networks. Unlike the then-standard circuit switching that required a dedicated connection, packet switching allowed data to be broken into packets and sent independently across the network.

During the 1970s and 1980s, the landscape of networking technology saw rapid advancements. Protocols such as TCP/IP emerged, becoming the backbone for reliable data transmission across increasingly complex networks. By 1983, ARPANET fully adopted TCP/IP, laying the groundwork for the modern Internet. This period also witnessed the rise of Local Area Networks (LANs), which linked computers within a restricted area, such as a building or campus, substantially boosting organizational productivity.

The early 1990s brought about another monumental change with Tim Berners-Lee's introduction of the World Wide Web, democratizing information access and transforming the internet from a specialized tool into a global utility. The web's graphical interface made the internet more accessible and appealing to the general public, catalyzing the explosive growth of network technology.

The turn of the millennium ushered in the era of wireless networking technologies, including Wi-Fi, facilitating internet access for mobile devices without the need for physical cables. The expansion of broadband technology also enhanced the speed and reliability of internet connections, supporting an array of digital content and services such as streaming video, cloud computing, and the proliferation of IoT devices.

Today, the evolution of network technology continues at an unprecedented pace. The advent of 5G wireless technology promises even faster speeds and more reliable connections, with the potential to revolutionize industries by enabling new services like remote surgery and autonomous vehicles. Furthermore, the ongoing developments in blockchain technology suggest a move towards more decentralized internet services, potentially transforming how data is managed and exchanged globally.

This ongoing evolution of network technology not only highlights technical advancements but also underscores the profound impact these innovations have had on reshaping societies and economies worldwide. As networks grow in complexity and significance, the future holds even more transformative potential.

1.3 Types of Networks: LAN, WAN, PAN, MAN

Here's a concise overview of the main network types and their specific applications:

Local Area Network (LAN): A LAN connects devices within a confined area, such as a building or campus, facilitating the sharing of resources like files and printers among a limited user base. This type of network is typically managed by a single organization and can be established using basic, cost-effective hardware such as Ethernet cables and network adapters.

Wide Area Network (WAN): Expansive in reach, a WAN encompasses larger geographical areas, connecting cities, regions, or countries. This network type is vital for organizations that operate over large distances, enabling the transmission of data across various locations. Unlike LANs, WANs generally utilize leased telecommunications circuits and require more complex equipment like routers to manage data flow across widespread areas.

Personal Area Network (PAN): Intended for personal use, a PAN operates within a small range, usually a few meters, connecting devices such as smartphones, laptops, and tablets. These networks can be either wired or wireless, using technologies like Bluetooth, and are ideal for personal device interconnectivity at home or while traveling.

Metropolitan Area Network (MAN): Bridging the gap between LANs and WANs, a MAN typically covers the area of a city and is used to connect multiple LANs within that geographical scope without relying on external telecommunication providers. Technologies employed may include Fiber Distributed Data Interface (FDDI) and Asynchronous Transfer Mode (ATM), offering efficient connectivity solutions for urban areas.

Each network type is designed to meet specific connectivity needs, from individual and local setups to expansive corporate communications across cities or even countries, ensuring appropriate scalability and efficient data distribution tailored to user requirements.

1.4 Essential Networking Terms

Networking entails a complex interplay of devices and protocols to ensure efficient communication and data transfer across different networks.

IP Address: Each device connected to a network is assigned a unique IP address, which uses a series of numbers divided by periods (IPv4) or colons (IPv6). This address identifies each device on the network, enabling precise routing of information.

Router: This device is crucial for directing data packets between and within networks. Routers analyze the destination addresses of incoming data and determine the most efficient path for the data to travel across the network.

Switch: Operating within a network, a switch connects various devices using their MAC addresses. It efficiently channels incoming data from one device to another within the same network by recognizing the specific hardware destination of each packet.

Firewall: A firewall is a type of security system that keeps an eye on and regulates inbound and outgoing network traffic in accordance with pre-established security rules. In order to prevent unwanted access, it serves as a barrier that separates trusted internal networks from untrusted external networks, such the internet.

Protocol: Protocols are the established rules that dictate the exchange and transmission of data between devices. Protocols like HTTP, FTP, and TCP/IP facilitate various functions and services on the network, ensuring that data is transferred reliably and securely.

Bandwidth: This therm refers to a network or internet connection's maximum data transfer rate. It is essential for figuring out the speed and capacity of network connections since it indicates how much data can be transferred over a particular connection in a specified amount of time.

Network Interface Card (NIC): This hardware component enables a computer or device to connect to a network. Whether integrated into the motherboard or installed as a separate component, the NIC plays a fundamental role in network communication.

Subnet Mask: Used in IP addressing, the subnet mask divides the IP address into network and host addresses, which helps in network organization and improves the efficiency of routing devices.

Gateway: Serving as a "gate" between networks, a gateway is a network node that routes data from a local network to other networks, facilitating data flow and communication between different network segments.

DNS (Domain Name System): This system translates more memorable domain names into numerical IP addresses needed for locating and identifying computer services and devices on underlying network protocols. It bridges the gap between user-friendliness and the technical needs of the network.

1.5 Overview of Networking Standards

Networking standards play a pivotal role in ensuring seamless interoperability, safety, and efficiency across diverse networking environments. These standards, established by a variety of influential organizations, enable hardware and software from different manufacturers to work together smoothly, which is critical for building and maintaining reliable network systems.

Key Organizations and Their Roles:

1. **IEEE (Institute of Electrical and Electronics Engineers):**

   - Known primarily for its development of network standards, IEEE has set numerous protocols under the IEEE 802 standard series, including Ethernet (802.3) and Wi-Fi (802.11). These standards are fundamental in local area networks (LANs) and metropolitan area networks (MANs), providing guidelines that facilitate data exchange and define network operations.

2. **IETF (Internet Engineering Task Force):**

   - This body plays a crucial role in the development of Internet standards, focusing on the Internet protocol suite (TCP/IP). The IETF is responsible for many foundational protocols such as the Simple Mail Transfer Protocol (SMTP) and the Domain Name System (DNS), which are integral to the functioning of the internet.

3. **ISO (International Organization for Standardization):**

   - In collaboration with the International Electrotechnical Commission (IEC), ISO develops wide-ranging standards, including those for the OSI (Open Systems Interconnection) model. The OSI model serves as a framework for understanding network interactions across seven layers, aiding in the systematic design and troubleshooting of network systems.

4. **ITU (International Telecommunication Union):**

   - As a specialized agency of the United Nations, ITU's role extends beyond traditional networking standards. It coordinates the global use of the radio spectrum, assists in the assignment of satellite orbits, supports telecommunication infrastructure development in the developing world, and fosters the establishment of worldwide standards to enable diverse communication systems to interconnect seamlessly.

5. **ANSI (American National Standards Institute):**

   - ANSI facilitates the creation and adoption of thousands of norms and guidelines that affect a multitude of sectors, including telecommunications and information technology. This organization helps ensure that network components like cables and connectors meet certain quality and safety standards, contributing to the overall reliability and security of network infrastructures.

By adhering to these standards, networking professionals ensure their systems are compatible with global network infrastructure, which is essential for supporting effective and secure communications and data exchange across different platforms and devices. Understanding and implementing these standards is crucial for anyone involved in the design, implementation, and maintenance of network systems.

1.6 The Role of Networking in Today's Tech Landscape

Networking fundamentally reshapes the technological landscape by providing the essential infrastructure that supports and drives modern digital and communication technologies.

Essential Connectivity and Accessibility: At its heart, networking facilitates the connectivity that fuels the internet, granting us access to information and resources from virtually anywhere in the world. This connectivity underpins cloud computing, enabling scalable access to computing services and resources online without the need for local infrastructure.

Support for Emerging Technologies: Networking is crucial for the functionality of cutting-edge technologies such as the Internet of Things (IoT), artificial intelligence (AI), and big data analytics. For example, IoT devices rely on networking to transmit vast amounts of data to cloud platforms where it can be processed and analyzed, supporting smarter decision-making and operations.

Enabling Remote Interactions: The shift towards remote work and learning, accelerated by global events, depends heavily on robust networking. Tools like video conferencing, real-time collaboration, and virtual classrooms rely on stable, high-speed internet connections, which are pivotal in maintaining productivity and accessibility to education.

Driving Economic Growth: Networking is a catalyst for economic development, enabling new business models and enhancing traditional ones. Industries such as e-commerce, online banking, and telemedicine rely on secure and efficient networks to operate globally, serving customers across various geographies and time zones.

Enhancing Personal Communication: Beyond its utility for business and education, networking enriches personal interactions. Platforms like social media, instant messaging, and emails rely on robust networking to help individuals maintain connections with family and friends, share life experiences, and build relationships, despite physical distances.

Addressing Security and Privacy: With the increasing integration of networking in daily life, security and privacy issues have become more prominent. Ensuring the protection of data as it traverses networks is crucial, leading to continuous advancements in cybersecurity protocols and measures aimed at safeguarding user privacy.

Chapter 2: Networking Hardware Essentials

2.1 The Function of Routers

Routers are integral to networking, serving as the backbone of internet connectivity by directing data packets across both local and multiple networks. These devices ensure that information is transmitted to its correct destination efficiently and accurately.

Traffic Management: Routers meticulously analyze network traffic, deciding the optimal pathways for data to travel. This decision-making process helps avoid potential congestion and is supported by sophisticated routing tables and protocols that track different paths, adapting to varying network conditions and prioritizing traffic as needed.

Inter-networking: A router's ability to link disparate networks into a cohesive system allows isolated networks to communicate with the broader internet. For example, a typical home router connects private local networks to the wider network of an internet service provider, thus integrating into the vast global network.

Network Address Translation (NAT): Routers often perform NAT to allow multiple devices on a private network to share a single IP address for internet access. This capability is vital for the efficient utilization of IP addresses, enabling several devices to access the internet simultaneously without requiring unique external IP addresses.

Security Measures: In addition to managing traffic, routers enhance network security. Many routers include built-in firewall capabilities, which monitor and control the flow of data in and out of the network to guard against cyber threats. Advanced routers may also support VPNs (Virtual Private Networks), providing encrypted connections for secure remote access.

Quality of Service (QoS): Routers are capable of prioritizing certain types of traffic over others, ensuring that critical services, such as VoIP (Voice over Internet Protocol) and multimedia streaming, receive the bandwidth necessary to function smoothly without disruption. This feature is crucial in both residential and commercial settings to maintain the quality of service that users expect and require.

2.2 Comparing Switches and Hubs

Switches and hubs are key elements of networking infrastructure, but they differ significantly in functionality, impacting network efficiency and performance.

Functionality and Data Handling: Hubs are simpler devices that connect Ethernet devices, causing them to act as a single network segment. They indiscriminately transmit data packets to all connected devices, regardless of the intended recipient. This can lead to data collisions and network congestion as the number of devices increases. Switches, by contrast, are more sophisticated; they manage data traffic efficiently by directing packets specifically to the intended recipient based on MAC addresses.

Traffic Management: Hubs broadcast incoming data packets to all ports, leading to unnecessary traffic and increased potential for collisions within the network. Switches streamline this process by maintaining a MAC address table, allowing them to send data directly to the correct port, thereby reducing unnecessary network traffic and minimizing collisions.

Performance: The operational differences between hubs and switches directly affect network performance. Switches enhance performance by reducing collision domains (each switch port is an independent collision domain) and directing data more accurately. This efficiency makes networks faster and more reliable compared to environments where hubs are used.

Security: From a security perspective, switches offer advantages over hubs because they can deliver packets directly to the intended recipient, which limits the chances of packet sniffing by unauthorized devices. In contrast, hubs broadcast all incoming packets across the network, potentially exposing data to all connected devices.

Use Cases: Hubs are suitable for small, simple networking setups where network performance, traffic, and security are not major concerns. They are less expensive and easier to configure than switches. Switches, however, are preferable in larger, more complex networks where bandwidth, performance, and security needs are greater.

2.3 Basics of Modems

Modems transform digital data from computers into analog signals suitable for transmission over these lines, and then reverse this process to interpret incoming analog signals back into digital form.

Modulation and Demodulation Explained: The term "modem" is a blend of 'modulator-demodulator'. This process involves converting the digital signals from a device into analog waves that can traverse conventional phone lines or similar analog paths. Upon reaching their destination, these signals undergo demodulation, where they're converted back from analog waves to a digital format that the receiving device can process and understand.

Diverse Types of Modems: Modems come in various forms, adapting to different types of connections:

- **Dial-up Modems:** These are the earliest type of modem used for home internet via standard telephone lines, offering limited connectivity speeds. They are largely obsolete in modern settings.

- **DSL Modems:** Utilizing existing telephone lines without disrupting voice services, DSL modems provide a much faster connection than their dial-up counterparts.

- **Cable Modems:** Operating over coaxial cables used for cable TV, these modems typically offer higher speed internet connections compared to DSL modems.

Crucial for Internet Connectivity: Modems are essential for accessing the Internet, particularly in settings that utilize broadband connections. They serve as the gateway between a user's local network and their internet service provider, linking through local telephone or cable lines.

Integration with Routers: In modern networking environments, modems often come integrated with routers in devices known as gateways. These combined devices streamline the setup and management of network connections by handling both signal conversion and data routing to various devices within a network.

Technological Progress: Technological advancements in modem technology, such as the implementation of DOCSIS (Data Over Cable Service Interface Specification) in cable modems, have dramatically enhanced the speed and reliability of internet connections, supporting the high demands of current internet usage.

2.4 Wireless Access Points Explained

Wireless Access Points (WAPs) are devices that bridge wireless-capable devices with a wired network through technologies like Wi-Fi or Bluetooth. These units extend the reach of a network to areas where physical wiring is challenging or unfeasible, thus enhancing the flexibility and mobility of device use across the space.

Core Functionality: Wireless Access Points connect directly to a network's router or switch via an Ethernet cable and broadcast a Wi-Fi signal within a specified area. This enables devices such as laptops, smartphones, and tablets to access the network wirelessly, thereby improving convenience and eliminating the need for direct, physical connections.

Deployment Considerations: In residential settings, a single WAP, often integrated into the router, generally suffices. However, larger spaces like offices or educational institutions may require multiple WAPs to ensure uniform wireless coverage throughout the premises, enabling seamless connectivity as users move around.

Network Management: Effective management of multiple WAPs is crucial. This includes strategic placement to prevent coverage overlap that can cause network congestion and slow speeds. Some networks employ a Wireless Distribution System (WDS) or mesh networking techniques, allowing WAPs to communicate directly with each other, facilitating smoother data packet transmission and enhancing network resilience.

Security Measures: Given the wireless nature of their transmission, securing WAPs is essential. They support various encryption protocols such as WEP, WPA, and WPA2 to secure data flows and restrict unauthorized access. With advancements in technology, WPA3 is becoming more common, offering superior security features to safeguard sensitive information.

Performance Influencers: The performance of WAPs can vary based on environmental conditions, the volume of connected devices, and the types of data transmitted. Optimal placement is key, avoiding interference from various electronic devices and physical barriers which could degrade signal strength.

Technological Advancements: Wireless technology continues to evolve, with newer WAPs supporting enhanced functionalities like MU-MIMO (Multi-User, Multiple Input, Multiple Output). This technology enables a WAP to handle communications with multiple devices simultaneously, significantly boosting network efficiency and capacity.

2.5 Security Appliances in Networks

Network security appliances are tools designed to safeguard the integrity, confidentiality, and availability of data within a network. These devices include a range of solutions such as firewalls, intrusion detection systems (IDS), intrusion prevention systems (IPS), and Unified Threat Management (UTM) systems, each playing a pivotal role in defending against diverse cyber threats.

Firewalls: Serving as the primary barrier against unauthorized access, firewalls manage both incoming and outgoing network traffic based on established security rules. Available as hardware-based, software-based, or hybrid solutions, firewalls scrutinize data packets to ensure they meet security standards before allowing them to pass through.

Intrusion Detection and Prevention Systems (IDS/IPS): IDS and IPS are critical in monitoring network traffic for abnormal activities that could indicate potential threats. While IDS systems generate alerts for network administrators to take action, IPS systems go a step further by actively blocking detected threats based on specific security policies.

Unified Threat Management (UTM): UTM systems offer a comprehensive security solution by integrating the functionalities of firewalls, IDS, and IPS, along with additional features like anti-virus, anti-spam, and content filtering. These devices simplify security management by consolidating multiple security functions into one platform, making it easier for administrators to oversee network security.

Virtual Private Networks (VPNs): VPN appliances are vital for creating secure communications over public networks, such as the internet. They encrypt data transmitted between remote users and the network, ensuring that sensitive information remains confidential and protected from interception.

Configuration and Management: Effective use of network security appliances requires meticulous configuration and ongoing management. This involves establishing robust security policies, keeping software and firmware up to date to guard against new threats, and consistently monitoring network traffic for signs of unusual or malicious activity.

Emerging Trends: The landscape of network security continues to evolve with technological advancements. Modern security appliances are increasingly incorporating artificial intelligence (AI) and machine learning (ML) to improve their ability to detect and respond to sophisticated cyber threats more effectively and proactively.

2.6 New Trends in Networking Hardware

The landscape of networking hardware is rapidly evolving, fueled by technological advances and a push for improved performance, security, and flexibility. Here's an exploration of the most influential trends currently reshaping this field:

1. Software-Defined Networking (SDN): SDN is revolutionizing network management by separating the control plane from the data plane. This architecture enables centralized management through SDN controllers, which streamline network design and operation by dynamically allocating resources based on demand. This flexibility allows organizations to adapt quickly to changing network requirements.

2. Network Function Virtualization (NFV): NFV is changing the deployment of network functions like routing, switching, and security, which traditionally required dedicated hardware. By virtualizing these functions, NFV allows them to be managed as software instances, reducing costs and enhancing deployment flexibility. This approach supports the rapid scaling of network services and improves operational agility.

3. 5G Technology: The deployment of 5G networks is a transformative trend in mobile connectivity, delivering faster data speeds and more reliable connections. Beyond enhancing consumer connectivity, 5G enables new applications in IoT, smart cities, and autonomous vehicles, which place increased demands on networking infrastructure.

4. Enhanced Wi-Fi Technologies: Technologies like Wi-Fi 6 are advancing wireless networking standards by improving speed, efficiency, and responsiveness. These innovations support higher throughput and reduced latency, catering to the needs of high-density environments and supporting a better user experience.

5. Internet of Things (IoT) Integration: With the proliferation of IoT devices, networking hardware is evolving to better manage increased device connectivity. This includes routers and access points designed to handle numerous connections simultaneously and incorporate robust security features to protect networks that integrate IoT devices.

6. Energy Efficiency: Energy efficiency is becoming a priority in networking hardware development, with manufacturers focusing on reducing the power consumption of devices. This shift is critical for minimizing both environmental impact and operational costs, particularly in data centers and large network infrastructures.

7. Advanced Security Features: As cyber threats grow in sophistication, networking hardware is being equipped with advanced security capabilities. Features like deep packet inspection, intrusion prevention systems, and advanced encryption are becoming standard to offer comprehensive protection against a wide array of cyber attacks.

These trends highlight the ongoing innovation within the networking sector, driven by both technological advancements and the evolving needs of businesses and consumers. As networks become increasingly complex and integral to various aspects of professional and personal life, the role of cutting-edge networking hardware in ensuring efficient, secure, and reliable connectivity is more crucial than ever.

Chapter 3: Designing Network Topologies

3.1 Understanding Network Topologies

A network topology dictates how different nodes and connections are arranged, impacting everything from performance to maintenance ease. Let's explore the fundamental network topologies, highlighting their unique benefits and limitations.

Bus Topology: Simple yet limited, a bus topology connects all devices via a single communication line known as a bus. This setup minimizes initial cabling costs and is straightforward to implement but suffers from scalability issues. Traffic congestion and data collisions are possible, and a single line failure can disrupt the entire network.

Star Topology: Commonly used due to its reliability, a star topology features a central hub or switch to which all network devices connect. This design facilitates easier management and troubleshooting, as each device operates independently of the others. However, the dependency on a central hub means that its failure can cripple the network.

Ring Topology: In this setup, each network device connects to two others, forming a circular data path. Ring topologies enhance data flow efficiency by preventing collisions through unidirectional traffic. Yet, the failure of a single link or device can disrupt the entire system, necessitating robust fault management strategies.

Mesh Topology: Offering the highest redundancy, mesh topologies connect each device directly to every other device. This design ensures network resilience, as multiple pathways can reroute data if one link fails. The complexity and cost of this topology, however, make it suitable primarily for networks where reliability is paramount.

Tree Topology: An extension of the star topology, tree topologies connect multiple star-configured networks to a central bus. This structure supports extensive scalability and is ideal for large, distributed networks. It combines the benefits of both star and bus topologies but requires careful planning to manage the inherent complexity.

Hybrid Topology: Tailored for specific needs, hybrid topologies combine elements of various topologies to leverage their strengths while mitigating their weaknesses. This approach is flexible and adaptable, making it ideal for complex or evolving network environments in large organizations.

3.2 Crafting a Network Layout

Creating an effective network layout goes beyond simply choosing a topology; it requires a nuanced approach to planning that carefully considers the specific requirements and limitations of the environment. Here's how this complex process unfolds:

Understanding and Addressing Network Requirements involves a deep dive into what the network must accomplish. This starts by identifying the types of services it will provide, such as internet access, VoIP, or data sharing, and understanding the applications it will support. The bandwidth needs, latency tolerance, and expected traffic volume are also critical factors that influence hardware choices and network design.

Selecting the Right Topology is crucial and depends on these requirements. For example, a star topology may be best for small offices that value ease of maintenance and simplicity, whereas a mesh topology could better serve a data center that requires high availability and resilience.

Ensuring Scalability and Flexibility in the design means planning for future growth and changes in technology. This might involve choosing modular hardware that can be easily upgraded or intentionally over-provisioning capacity to accommodate future needs.

Optimizing the Physical Layout of the network takes into account the actual environment where the network will be deployed. It's about strategically placing cables, network devices, and workstations to reduce cable lengths and interference, ensuring all areas are adequately covered.

Integrating Redundancy and Failover capabilities are vital for maintaining network reliability. This could mean installing additional cabling, using dual-homed connections for critical devices, or including redundant power supplies to prevent failures from disrupting the network.

Documenting the Design thoroughly is another critical step. Creating detailed diagrams, recording IP addressing schemes, and noting configuration details are essential for effective future troubleshooting and maintenance.

Validating the Design with Simulation Tools before actual deployment helps anticipate potential issues by simulating traffic flows, network loads, and the impact of changes. This preemptive step can save considerable time and resources.

Implementing and Testing the Network carefully once the design is validated ensures that the network fulfills all performance, functionality, and security requirements as expected. This phase may involve adjustments and optimizations based on real-world performance and user feedback.

3.3 Design for Scalability and Flexibility

Designing a network to be both scalable and flexible is vital for accommodating organizational growth and evolving technology.

Employing a Modular Design: Structuring your network in modular segments allows for easier management and future expansion. By organizing the network into repeatable, manageable units, such as standardized racks in data centers, expansion becomes as simple as integrating additional racks. This modular setup minimizes disruptions to existing operations while facilitating growth.

Implementing a Layered Architecture: A traditional three-layer model, which includes the distribution, core , and access layers, supports independent scalability. You can expand each layer by adding more devices or connections, which allows for growth without compromising the integrity of the network.

Building a High-capacity Backbone: To prepare for increased data traffic, it's crucial to establish a robust network core with high-capacity and high-speed capabilities. Opting for high-speed interfaces and fiber-optic cables ensures that the backbone can support growing data demands, making the network future-proof.

Utilizing Virtualization: Network virtualization detaches the physical hardware from the network services it hosts, offering enhanced flexibility. Virtual networks can be quickly reconfigured or resized according to changing demands without the need to physically alter the hardware setup.

Integrating Cloud Services: Incorporating cloud solutions into the network design offers scalable and flexible resource management. Cloud services can be adjusted according to demand, providing not only scalability but also enhanced redundancy and disaster recovery options.

Adjusting Quality of Service (QoS) Settings: By implementing Quality of Service mechanisms, you can ensure that critical network traffic is prioritized, maintaining performance standards during peak periods. As network usage evolves, QoS settings can be adjusted to continue meeting the bandwidth needs of essential applications.

Staying Current with Emerging Technologies: Keeping abreast of new technologies and standards, such as the latest Wi-Fi 6E or upcoming 5G advancements, prepares the network to support new devices and applications, ensuring long-term relevance.

Conducting Regular Network Assessments: Continuously monitoring network performance and capacity allows for ongoing adjustments and improvements. Implementing a cycle of regular assessments and updates ensures the network remains optimized and responsive to new challenges and opportunities.

3.4 Physical vs. Logical Topology Differences

In network design, understanding the distinctions between physical and logical topologies is fundamental, as each provides unique perspectives on the network's structure and functionality.

Physical Topology: Physical topology refers to the tangible aspects of a network—how the cables, devices, and other hardware are arranged. It details the physical connections and geographic placements of all components like routers, switches, and hubs. This topology is crucial for the physical maintenance of the network, helping with tasks such as installation of cables, network troubleshooting, and managing the hardware components. It provides a clear map for the setup and connectivity of the network's physical infrastructure.

Logical Topology: Contrasting with physical topology, logical topology deals with how data flows across the network irrespective of the physical layout. It's more about the paths that data takes and how the network devices communicate with each other through those paths. Logical topology focuses on aspects like signal paths, protocols, and data transfer patterns across the network. This topology is vital for network administration as it influences data routing decisions, network traffic management, and overall network performance optimization.

Key Differences and Their Impact on Network Management:

- **Visualization:** Physical topology can typically be seen and touched, making it straightforward to identify. Logical topology, however, often requires specific software to map out data flow paths, making it less tangible.

- **Flexibility:** Logical topologies offer greater flexibility than physical topologies. Adjustments in logical setups, like altering protocols or IP configurations, can be done without physical changes to the network, facilitating easier updates and adaptations.

- **Network Performance:** The efficiency of data pathways defined by the logical topology directly impacts the network's performance. For instance, in a logical ring topology, the slow processing speed of one node could degrade the performance, regardless of a robust physical setup.

- **Troubleshooting:** Troubleshooting physical topology issues might involve addressing faulty cables or malfunctioning hardware, whereas logical topology problems could relate to software configurations, routing protocols, or corrupt data packets.

3.5 Challenges and Solutions in Network Design

Network design involves navigating various challenges that span technical, strategic, and operational aspects. Effectively addressing these challenges requires a blend of advanced technological solutions, strategic foresight, and adaptability. Here's a more integrated overview of these challenges and the corresponding solutions to ensure a robust network design:

Scalability Challenges: Networks need to expand seamlessly as organizational needs grow. The key to scalability lies in adopting a modular design approach, where the network is built in manageable segments that can be expanded as needed without major overhauls. Utilizing technologies like Software-Defined Networking (SDN) and cloud services also supports scalability, as they allow for flexible resource management and quick adaptation to increased demands.

Security Concerns: As networks expand and become more complex, they also become more vulnerable to internal and external security threats. To safeguard networks, implementing layered security measures is critical. This includes deploying firewalls, intrusion detection systems (IDS), and conducting regular security audits. End-to-end encryption for data in transit and stringent access controls further bolster network security, protecting sensitive data and infrastructure from unauthorized access.

Managing Network Congestion and Reliability: Network traffic management is crucial to prevent congestion and ensure reliable service. Quality of Service (QoS) protocols can be used to prioritize essential traffic and manage bandwidth effectively, ensuring that critical applications always have the necessary resources. Additionally, incorporating redundant connections and backup hardware can help maintain network services even during system failures.

Cost Management: Balancing financial constraints with the need for robust networking capabilities is a constant challenge. By optimizing the use of existing resources through technologies like virtualization and cloud computing, organizations can reduce costs. Careful planning of new technology investments to ensure they provide tangible benefits is also essential.

Integrating New Technologies: Integrating new technologies without disrupting existing operations requires careful planning. Using APIs and maintaining standard protocols helps ensure that new systems are compatible with existing ones. Effective change management processes are also crucial to smoothly transition as new technologies are incorporated.

Performance Optimization: To ensure optimal network performance under various conditions, continuous monitoring is essential. Using network performance monitoring tools helps identify and address issues proactively. Adjusting configurations based on these insights ensures that the network consistently meets performance standards.

Complexity Management: As networks grow, so does their complexity. Simplifying network management through centralized control mechanisms and automation can help. Network management software and AI-driven tools can reduce the burden of routine tasks, making it easier to manage complex networks efficiently.

Compliance with Regulations: Compliance with legal and regulatory requirements is mandatory and can vary significantly by region and industry. Staying informed about relevant regulations and incorporating compliance into network design and operations is crucial. Regular reviews and updates to the network help ensure ongoing compliance.

3.6 Case Studies on Effective Network Design

To illustrate the principles of effective network design, here are several case studies that highlight how different organizations successfully implemented advanced network strategies to meet their unique needs:

Global Retail Corporation:

Challenge: A large retail corporation needed to ensure reliable, secure communication across its global network, including retail stores, warehouses, and regional headquarters.

Solution: The corporation implemented a hybrid WAN (Wide Area Network), utilizing MPLS (Multiprotocol Label Switching) for critical traffic and broadband connections for less critical data. This strategy enhanced both cost efficiency and network resilience.

Outcome: The result was significantly improved operational efficiency and reduced downtime, alongside enhanced disaster recovery capabilities, supporting smooth and continuous global operations.

University Campus Network:

Challenge: A university struggled with network congestion during peak usage times, exacerbated by high bandwidth demands from video streaming and large file downloads.

Solution: The university revamped its network architecture, adopting a tiered design with high-performance core switches and distributed access points. It also implemented SDN (Software-Defined Networking) to enforce application-aware network policies, prioritizing academic resources.

Outcome: This led to a more stable network during peak usage, prioritized access to educational materials, and improved overall user satisfaction across the campus.

Healthcare Provider:

Challenge: A healthcare network required a system that upheld high security and compliance with health data regulations, while facilitating fast access to patient records across various locations.

Solution: The solution was a mesh network topology with high redundancy and robust security protocols, including advanced encryption and intrusion prevention systems. Network functions were managed more flexibly via NFV (Network Function Virtualization).

Outcome: The network achieved compliance with health data protection standards and enhanced the security and accessibility of patient records, ensuring reliable and secure health services.

Tech Startup:

Challenge: A rapidly expanding tech startup needed a highly scalable network that could adapt quickly to new additions of employees and services without major reconfigurations.

Solution: The startup integrated cloud-based services with on-premises SDN, facilitating easy scalability and network management. This included automated provisioning of network resources through the cloud.

Outcome: The company enjoyed rapid scaling of operations and resources, allowing for swift adaptation to business needs with minimal investment in physical infrastructure.

Financial Services Firm:

Challenge: A financial services firm required a network capable of handling high-volume, latency-sensitive trading applications, while ensuring utmost security and data integrity.

Solution: The firm set up a high-speed, ultra-low latency network using fiber optic technology directly connected to trading platforms and financial exchanges, complemented by comprehensive security measures including real-time monitoring and anomaly detection.

Outcome: This network design not only improved transaction speeds and reduced latency but also significantly strengthened network security, bolstering the firm's competitive edge in financial services.

These case studies demonstrate that with thoughtful network design and strategic implementation of technology, organizations can overcome diverse challenges and significantly enhance their operational effectiveness.

Chapter 4: Protocols and Networking Models

4.1 Exploring the OSI Model

The Open Systems Interconnection (OSI) Model, established by the International Organization for Standardization (ISO) in the 1970s, serves as a conceptual framework that delineates network interactions across seven distinct tiers. This model is crucial for standardizing communications across different systems and networks, offering a structured environment where each tier has a specific role and interacts seamlessly with the tiers above and below it.

Physical Tier (Tier 1): This foundational tier manages the raw transmission and reception of the unstructured data stream across a physical medium. It encompasses everything related to the physical network connections like the cables (e.g., fiber, Ethernet) and hardware components such as switches and network interface cards (NICs), handling the electrical and mechanical aspects that underpin the physical connections in networking.

Data Link Tier (Tier 2): Building on the physical tier, the data link tier ensures reliable node-to-node data transfer. It manages the direct links between nodes that are directly connected, handling error correction from the physical tier, ensuring proper flow control, and synchronizing frames, which are the protocol data units at this tier.

Network Tier (Tier 3): This tier is responsible for the routing of data packets across potentially multiple and diverse networks via routers. Key functions include addressing and routing, which involves determining the optimal path across a complex series of networks, and managing traffic to prevent bottlenecks.

Transport Tier (Tier 4): The transport tier oversees the delivery of data between systems and is crucial for managing end-to-end data transmission services. It provides reliable data transfer services to the upper tiers by handling error recovery and flow control, ensuring that data is completely and accurately transferred.

Session Tier (Tier 5): This tier establishes, manages, and terminates connections between applications. It coordinates communication between systems, managing sessions by initiating, controlling, and ending the exchanges of information among communicating systems.

Presentation Tier (Tier 6): Acting as a translator, this tier formats or translates data from the application tier into a suitable form for transmission or from the network up to the application tier. It handles encryption and decryption required by the application tier as well as data compression, ensuring that data is presented in a way that can be understood by the receiving end.

Application Tier (Tier 7): The application tier is the closest to the end user and interacts directly with software applications to manage network processes. It provides essential services such as email, file transfer, and other client-server or peer-to-peer processes, facilitating end-user services directly.

4.2 Insights into the TCP/IP Model

The Transmission Control Protocol/Internet Protocol (TCP/IP) model, developed in the 1970s by Vint Cerf and Bob Kahn, is a core framework that dictates how data is transmitted over the internet. It streamlines communication processes into four essential layers, making it practical and robust for internet functioning, unlike the seven-layer OSI model.

Link Layer (Network Interface Layer): This layer blends the physical and data link layers of the OSI model, handling both the physical hardware connections and the logical data exchange mechanisms. It ensures that data can be passed between the network and end systems using technologies like Ethernet and PPP, along with necessary hardware drivers.

Internet Layer (Network Layer): Serving a similar purpose as the OSI model's network layer, this layer manages the logistics of data routing, ensuring packets are sent from the source to the destination across various networks. Protocols such as IP and ICMP are crucial here, managing traffic with functions like addressing and forwarding.

Transport Layer: This layer parallels its OSI counterpart in functionality. It manages the end-to-end communication session between hosts, emphasizing reliable data transmission. TCP is used for reliable connections, ensuring data integrity and order, while UDP supports quicker, connectionless communication without guaranteed delivery.

Application Layer: Operating at the top level, this layer handles the network services that facilitate applications. It is involved with defining protocols such as HTTP, FTP, SMTP, and DNS that help applications interface effectively with the network.

The TCP/IP model is geared towards practical, real-world application, emphasizing efficient internetworking and problem-solving in network communication. This focus on functionality rather than theoretical structure makes it foundational for anyone involved in network design or management, particularly within environments that rely heavily on TCP/IP for communications. Understanding this model is essential for ensuring that networks are not only effective at data transmission but also robust, scalable, and adaptable to new technologies.

4.3 Key Network Protocols and Their Functions

Network protocols are standardized rules that guide how data is communicated across different devices within a network. Each protocol is tailored to address specific parts of the communication process, facilitating both efficient and secure data transfers. Here's an overview of several key network protocols and their primary roles:

HTTP and HTTPS: HTTP is pivotal for web communications, forming the basis of data exchange on the World Wide Web. It specifies how messages should be formatted and transmitted, and how web servers and browsers should respond to various commands. HTTPS enhances HTTP by encrypting the data to secure transactions, crucial for safe browsing and online transactions.

FTP: The File Transfer Protocol is used for transferring files between computers on a network, allowing users to download and upload files. This is particularly useful for handling large files and managing remote server files.

SMTP: The Simple Mail Transfer Protocol is fundamental for email transmission across the Internet. It handles the sending of emails and works in conjunction with IMAP or POP3, which retrieve emails at the user's end.

TCP and IP: The duo of TCP/IP protocols underpins most internet-based communications. TCP ensures reliable data transmission between devices by managing packet delivery, while IP takes care of addressing and routing the data packets across different network paths.

DNS: The Domain Name System is a protocol that translates human-friendly domain names into IP addresses that networking equipment need for locating and identifying devices and services on the internet.

DHCP: The Dynamic Host Configuration Protocol significantly simplifies network management by automatically assigning IP addresses and other important network settings to devices, allowing them to communicate effectively on the network without manual configuration.

SSH: Secure Shell provides a secure channel for network administrators to access computers over an insecure network. It ensures secure log-ins, secure file transfers, and safe execution of commands on remote computers.

SNMP: The Simple Network Management Protocol is used by network administrators for network management, monitoring network performance, and detecting network faults or configuration issues in devices like servers, printers, and routers.

4.4 Comprehensive Guide to Protocol Suites

Protocol suites are collections of network protocols that ensure various hardware and software from different manufacturers can interact seamlessly. Here's a more integrated look into the primary protocol suites that shape networking:

TCP/IP Suite: The TCP/IP suite is fundamental to internet networking, serving as the primary architecture that supports global internet operations. It encompasses a variety of protocols that handle tasks ranging from routing and addressing with IP to ensuring reliable data transmission with TCP. This suite is pivotal for the basic functionalities of networking such as routing data across different networks, managing errors, and checking connectivity.

OSI Suite: While the OSI model itself is not a suite used in practical networking, it offers an educational framework for understanding network layer interactions and is often referenced for theoretical purposes. Protocols associated with the OSI model, like X.25 or TP4, are primarily used for academic exploration.

AppleTalk: AppleTalk was historically significant for Apple environments, simplifying networking functions like file sharing and network printing on early Macintosh computers. Though it has become largely obsolete, AppleTalk's suite included several layers of protocols that once provided basic network services efficiently.

IPX/SPX Suite: Favored in networks running the Novell NetWare operating systems, the IPX/SPX suite was celebrated for its straightforward approach to routing and data transmission. IPX managed addressing and routing, while SPX handled connection-oriented services, offering a simple yet effective networking solution.

NetBIOS/NetBEUI: Developed by IBM for small-scale PC networks, the NetBIOS/NetBEUI suite supported essential networking functions like file and printer sharing within local area networks (LANs). Although limited in scale and scope, it was well-suited for small network environments during its prime.

Integration and Compatibility: In modern networks that often blend new technologies with legacy systems, integrating various protocol suites is crucial. Techniques like gateways, encapsulation, and tunneling are employed to ensure seamless communication across different network protocols, supporting smooth and efficient network operations.

4.5 Setting Up and Configuring Protocols

Setting up and configuring network protocols is a critical task in network management, ensuring that communication and data transfer across the network are conducted smoothly and securely. Here's a guide on how to effectively set up and configure various network protocols:

1. Determine Requirements:

- Before configuring any protocols, it's essential to understand the network's requirements. This includes identifying the types of devices involved, the nature of the data being transferred, security needs, and performance expectations.

2. Choose Appropriate Protocols:

- Based on the requirements, select protocols that best fit the network's needs. For instance, TCP/IP is suitable for reliable communication, while UDP might be chosen for real-time applications where speed is more critical than reliability.

3. Configuration Tools and Software:

- Use network configuration tools and software to set protocols. This can include network management systems, command-line interfaces (CLI), or graphical user interfaces (GUI) provided by network device vendors.

4. Configure Network Addressing:

- Set up IP addressing schemes, including subnetting and assigning static or dynamic IP addresses using DHCP. Ensure that the addressing scheme aligns with the network's scale and segmentation needs.

5. Set Routing Protocols:

- Configure routing protocols to manage how routers communicate with each other and route traffic. Common routing protocols include RIP, OSPF, and BGP, each suitable for different network scales and topologies.

6. Configure Switching Protocols:

- In environments with switches, set up VLANs (Virtual Local Area Networks) and STP (Spanning Tree Protocol) to manage data paths and avoid loops within the network.

7. Implement Security Protocols:

- Secure network communications by configuring security protocols such as SSL/TLS for encryption, SSH for secure remote access, and setting up firewalls and access control lists (ACLs) to regulate traffic.

8. Quality of Service (QoS):

- Configure QoS settings to prioritize traffic. This is crucial for ensuring that critical applications, such as VoIP and video conferencing, receive the necessary bandwidth and latency requirements.

9. Testing and Validation:

- After configuration, thoroughly test the network to ensure all protocols are functioning correctly. Use tools like packet sniffers and network analyzers to monitor traffic and identify any misconfigurations or bottlenecks.

10. Documentation and Maintenance:

- Document all configurations for future reference and troubleshooting. Regularly review and update the configurations to adapt to network changes and technological advancements.

11. Training and Compliance:

- Ensure that network administrators are trained on the protocols in use and that protocol configurations comply with relevant standards and policies.

4.6 Troubleshooting Common Protocol Issues

Troubleshooting protocol issues is a critical skill for network administrators, as these issues can significantly impact network performance and reliability. Here are common protocol-related problems and strategies for diagnosing and resolving them:

1. Connectivity Issues:

- **Symptoms:** Devices cannot connect to the network, intermittent connectivity, or no internet access.

- **Common Causes:** Misconfigured IP settings, DHCP issues, or DNS resolution problems.

- **Troubleshooting Steps:** Verify IP configuration settings, ensure DHCP servers are functioning correctly, and check DNS settings and connectivity with tools like **ping** and **nslookup**.

2. Slow Network Performance:

- **Symptoms:** Slow data transfer rates, long page load times, video buffering.

- **Common Causes:** Congestion, incorrect QoS configurations, or inefficient routing protocols.

- **Troubleshooting Steps:** Check bandwidth utilization and prioritize traffic using QoS settings. Adjust routing protocols and configurations as necessary.

3. Routing Failures:

- **Symptoms:** Data packets fail to reach their destination, resulting in dropped connections or network outages.

- **Common Causes:** Incorrect routing tables, misconfigured gateways, or failed routers.

- **Troubleshooting Steps:** Verify routing tables and settings on routers, use traceroute to identify where packets are being dropped, and ensure all routers and gateways are configured correctly.

4. Protocol Configuration Errors:

- **Symptoms:** Network devices fail to communicate effectively, leading to network errors or suboptimal performance.

- **Common Causes:** Incorrect protocol settings, incompatible protocol versions, or erroneous network policies.

- **Troubleshooting Steps:** Review and validate protocol configurations across devices. Ensure that all devices are using compatible versions and settings align with network policies.

5. Security Breaches:

- **Symptoms:** Unauthorized access, data breaches, or suspicious network activity.

- **Common Causes:** Weak encryption, poor authentication practices, or compromised security protocols like outdated SSL/TLS versions.

- **Troubleshooting Steps:** Update to the latest security protocols and encryption standards, strengthen authentication mechanisms, and monitor network traffic for unusual patterns.

6. Hardware-Related Protocol Issues:

- **Symptoms:** Network crashes, hardware malfunctions, or specific devices being unable to communicate on the network.

- **Common Causes:** Faulty network interface cards (NICs), outdated firmware, or physical damage impacting protocol operations.

- **Troubleshooting Steps:** Replace or repair faulty hardware, update firmware, and ensure that hardware is compatible with the network's protocols.

7. VoIP Quality Issues:

- **Symptoms:** Poor call quality, dropped calls, or delays in VoIP communications.

- **Common Causes:** Misconfigured SIP or RTP protocols, insufficient bandwidth, or improper QoS settings.

- **Troubleshooting Steps:** Check and configure SIP and RTP settings, ensure adequate bandwidth is available, and configure QoS to prioritize VoIP traffic.

Effective troubleshooting involves a systematic approach to identifying the source of the problem and applying the appropriate solutions. Using network monitoring tools and diagnostic commands can help in quickly pinpointing issues and restoring network functionality. Regular training and updates on the latest network technologies and protocols are also vital in preventing protocol issues and enhancing network reliability.

Chapter 5: IP Addressing Fundamentals

5.1 Introduction to IP Addressing

IP addressing is a fundamental component of network communications, ensuring that every device connected to a network can be uniquely identified and can communicate effectively. Whether in local networks or across the vast reaches of the Internet, IP addresses play a pivotal role.

Understanding the Basics of IP Addresses: IP addresses come in two main versions, each with a unique format:

- **IPv4:** This version uses a 32-bit address format, typically shown as four decimal numbers separated by dots, like 192.168.1.1. Each segment of the address can range from 0 to 255.

- **IPv6:** To accommodate a growing need for more IP addresses, IPv6 uses a 128-bit address system, displayed as eight groups of four hexadecimal digits separated by colons, such as 2001:0db8:85a3:0000:0000:0a0e:0000:0000. This expansion allows for a vastly increased number of addresses.

The Role of IP Addresses:

- **Routing:** IP addresses are essential for routing data packets between devices on a network and across the internet. Routers use these addresses to determine the most efficient path for sending data to its destination.

- **Network Interface Identification:** Each device on a network must have a unique IP address to participate in network communications, ensuring that data sent across a network reaches the correct destination.

Dynamic and Static IP Addressing:

- **Static IP Addressing:** Some devices require a fixed IP address that does not change, such as servers or network printers. These devices use static IP addresses that are manually assigned and remain constant.

- **Dynamic IP Addressing:** Most devices use dynamic IP addressing, where IP addresses are assigned by the Dynamic Host Configuration Protocol (DHCP). This method allows addresses to be reused and dynamically assigned to devices as they connect and disconnect from the network, simplifying address management and optimizing resource usage.

Importance of IP Addressing:

- **Connectivity:** IP addresses are crucial for the basic connectivity of devices on a network, enabling communication between diverse devices and network segments.

- **Network Security:** In network security, IP addresses help identify devices and manage access to network resources. IP address filtering can restrict access to certain users based on their IP address, enhancing security measures.

5.2 Differences Between IPv4 and IPv6

The evolution from IPv4 to IPv6 marks a transformation in internet technology, primarily driven by the need for a significantly larger address space to support the burgeoning number of devices online. Here's an exploration of the fundamental differences between these two Internet Protocol versions:

Address Space:

- **IPv4:** Initially, IPv4's approximately 4.3 billion unique addresses seemed ample, but the exponential growth of the internet and connected devices quickly outstripped this supply.

- **IPv6:** With about 340 undecillion addresses available, IPv6 offers a virtually unlimited address pool, ensuring the capacity to support global internet growth for many generations.

Header Simplification:

- **IPv4:** The IPv4 header includes 14 fields, some of which are often unused and can slow down packet processing.

- **IPv6:** IPv6 simplifies this with a streamlined header that contains only 8 fields, enhancing processing efficiency.

Autoconfiguration:

- **IPv4:** Configuring network addresses with IPv4 can require manual setup or the use of additional protocols like DHCP.

- **IPv6:** IPv6 supports stateless address autoconfiguration (SLAAC), enabling devices to automatically generate an IP address when connecting to a network, simplifying network configuration.

Network Security:

- **IPv4:** Security in IPv4 is not integrated into the protocol itself; it requires additional configurations and the use of protocols like IPSec.

- **IPv6:** Designed with security as a core feature, IPv6 mandates the implementation of IPSec, bolstering data confidentiality, authenticity, and integrity.

Handling Network Broadcasts:

- **IPv4:** Utilizes broadcast addresses that send data to all network nodes, potentially leading to congestion.

- **IPv6:** Replaces broadcasts with multicast to specific groups of devices, reducing unnecessary traffic and improving network efficiency.

Support for Mobility and Multicast:

- **IPv4:** While it supports basic multicast, IPv4 lacks robust features for modern mobile networking.

- **IPv6:** Enhances support for mobile IP and multicast, aiding efficient network management and device mobility.

The transition to IPv6 not only addresses the limitations in address space found with IPv4 but also brings advancements in routing, network configuration, and security, making it essential for the sustainable growth of the Internet.

5.3 Techniques for Effective Subnetting

Subnetting is a practice in network management that segments a larger network into smaller, more manageable logical units called subnets. This strategy not only improves network efficiency and security but also facilitates better traffic management. Here's how to approach effective subnetting:

Understanding Subnet Masks: A subnet mask is critical as it determines how the IP address is divided into network and host portions. Adjusting the subnet mask affects the number of available host addresses within each subnet. For instance, changing a subnet mask from 255.255.255.0 to 255.255.255.192 reduces the number of host addresses per subnet but increases the total number of subnets.

Defining Network Requirements: It's essential to start with a clear understanding of your network needs, such as how many subnets are required and the number of hosts in each subnet. This step guides how you allocate bits in your subnet mask and structure your network efficiently.

Employing CIDR: Classless Inter-Domain Routing (CIDR) replaces older class-based addressing, allowing for variable-length subnet masks that provide greater flexibility and more efficient use of IP address space. For example, the notation 192.168.1.0/24 indicates that the network portion of the address occupies the first 24 bits.

IP Address Allocation: Allocate IP addresses strategically within subnets to maximize operational efficiency. Place hosts that frequently interact in the same subnet to reduce inter-subnet traffic, which can enhance performance and reduce router load.

Planning for Growth: Design subnets with expansion in mind, ensuring there's sufficient address space to accommodate growth without the need for future restructuring.

Utilizing Tools and Software: Tools such as subnet calculators and network management software can simplify the subnetting process, helping ensure accuracy and efficiency in subnet configuration and management.

Regular Reviews and Adjustments: Continually monitor your subnet usage and performance. As your network evolves and expands, adjustments to your subnetting strategy might be necessary to maintain efficiency.

Hierarchical Subnetting: For larger networks, consider hierarchical subnetting, which involves creating layers of subnets. This can simplify routing complexity and improve overall network performance.

Integrating Security Measures: Subnetting can also enhance network security. By isolating segments of your network, you can contain threats and control access to sensitive areas more effectively.

5.4 Managing IP Address Allocation

Effectively managing IP address allocation is crucial for maintaining network efficiency and ensuring reliable and secure communication across devices. Here's how to strategically handle IP address distribution:

Centralized Management through DHCP: Using Dynamic Host Configuration Protocol (DHCP) allows for the automatic assignment of IP addresses, making management simpler and more efficient. DHCP servers not only distribute IP addresses but also manage network configuration details like default gateways and DNS servers, reducing the need for manual setup on each device.

Strategic Address Space Planning: Subnetting is an essential technique that breaks down a larger network into smaller sub-networks, enhancing both performance and IP address efficiency. It's important to plan these subnets carefully to avoid address conflicts and ensure each subnet has adequate addresses for current and future needs.

Maintaining Documentation and Records: Implementing an IP Address Management (IPAM) system is beneficial for tracking and organizing IP addresses. Such systems help in maintaining clear records of address allocation and can simplify troubleshooting and enhance network security.

Reserving IP Addresses: Certain devices like servers and network printers should have static IP addresses due to their critical role in network operations. For devices that need consistent IP addresses but not necessarily static ones, DHCP reservations can be useful. This method reserves an IP address for a device based on its MAC address, ensuring it receives the same IP address each time it connects to the network.

Regular Monitoring and Auditing: Conducting regular audits helps ensure that IP address allocations adhere to network policies and helps in spotting any irregularities or unauthorized devices. Analyzing how IP addresses are utilized can reveal underused subnets or exhausted IP ranges, providing insights for better subnet management and address allocation.

Ensuring Scalability and Flexibility: Networks must be adaptable to changes such as organizational expansions or reductions, which might necessitate adjustments to the IP addressing scheme. Preparing for such changes ensures that the network can evolve without significant disruptions.

Preparing for IPv6 Integration: With IPv4 addresses becoming scarce, planning for IPv6 integration is essential. IPv6 offers a much larger address space and requires careful planning and phased implementation to ensure a smooth transition.

Securing IP Allocation Processes: Protecting the DHCP servers and the overall IP allocation process is vital. Implement security practices like DHCP snooping and dynamic ARP inspection to defend against unauthorized access and attacks.

5.5 The Function of NAT in Networks

Network Address Translation (NAT) plays a pivotal role in both residential and corporate network environments, enhancing security and managing limited IP address spaces effectively. Here's a breakdown of how NAT functions and its significance in network operations:

Conservation of IP Addresses: NAT facilitates address multiplexing, which allows multiple devices on a private network to share a single public IP address for internet access. This strategy is essential for conserving the globally limited pool of IPv4 addresses, helping to extend the usable life of IPv4 in the face of address exhaustion.

Enhancing Routing and Network Security: NAT enhances security by implementing a form of security through obscurity; it masks internal IP addresses from the external network. This makes it more difficult for external threats to directly target internal devices. Additionally, NAT often functions at the network gateway, efficiently managing incoming and outgoing traffic and adding an extra layer of security.

Different Types of NAT:

- **Dynamic NAT** assigns a public IP address from a pool of available addresses to a private IP address on an as-needed basis.

- **Static NAT** links one private IP address to one public IP address, commonly used in scenarios like web hosting from a private network.

- **Port Address Translation (PAT)** allows multiple private IP addresses to share one or a few public IP addresses using different ports. This type is prevalent in small to medium-sized business settings.

Configuration and Management: Configuring NAT requires setting up policies and rules on network devices like routers or firewalls that support NAT functionality. These rules define which addresses need translation and the type of NAT to apply. Special attention is needed for protocols that embed IP addresses in the data packet's payload since NAT typically only modifies the packet's header.

Challenges and Considerations: While NAT offers many benefits, it can also introduce complexities in network configuration and minor delays due to the translation process. Some applications and protocols that depend on end-to-end connectivity might face compatibility issues with NAT, necessitating specific configurations or alternative approaches.

Transition to IPv6: As the newer IPv6 gains traction, offering a vast address space that allows every device to have its public IP address, the necessity for NAT diminishes. However, NAT remains relevant in transitional architectures where IPv4 and IPv6 coexist, ensuring smooth operation across mixed-environment networks.

5.6 Advanced Strategies for IP Address Management

As networks expand and become more complex, the management of IP addresses must also evolve to address the growing challenges. Advanced IP Address Management (IPAM) strategies are essential for maintaining efficient network operation, enhancing security, and ensuring reliability. Here's a closer look at sophisticated strategies for managing IP addresses effectively:

Utilizing IPAM Software: IPAM software is invaluable for centralizing the management of IP addresses. These tools automate the tracking and managing of all IP-related configurations, such as DHCP leases, DNS settings, and detailed subnet usage, which not only reduces human error but also lowers operational costs. Modern IPAM software also includes capabilities for real-time tracking, historical analysis of IP usage, and proactive alerts about network anomalies like subnet capacity limits or IP conflicts.

Integration with Network Operations: By integrating IPAM with existing network monitoring and configuration management tools, you can automate numerous network management tasks. For instance, when a device joins the network, the IPAM system can automatically assign an IP address, update DNS records, and enforce access controls, all based on predefined network policies. This seamless integration helps streamline network operations and ensures consistency across network management tasks.

Advanced Subnetting and Segmentation: Efficient use of subnetting can enhance network performance and security. Organizing subnets logically—by department, geographic location, or application type—can optimize traffic flow and minimize risks. Employing a hierarchical IP addressing structure that reflects the organization's layout simplifies the management and scalability of the network.

Supporting IPv6 Transition: As the internet continues transitioning to IPv6, it's crucial to manage this shift thoughtfully. Implementing dual-stack systems allows networks to support both IPv4 and IPv6 simultaneously, facilitating a smoother transition. Thoroughly planning your IPv6 address scheme is also critical, as it should accommodate future expansions without the need for frequent changes.

Security and Compliance: Regular audits of IP addresses ensure that only authorized devices access the network, enhancing security. Additionally, maintaining rigorous access control to IPAM tools, encrypting data involved in IP management tasks, and ensuring compliance with organizational policies are all vital for safeguarding network integrity.

Disaster Recovery and Business Continuity: It's essential to have redundancy within the IPAM systems to prevent single points of failure. Regular backups of IPAM data and configurations enable quick restoration following any system failure, ensuring business continuity.

By adopting these advanced strategies, organizations can not only manage their IP address spaces more effectively but also enhance overall network security and operational efficiency. This proactive approach to IP address management is essential for keeping up with the demands of modern network environments.

Chapter 6: Essential Network Services

6.1 Understanding DNS and DHCP

Domain Name System (DNS) and Dynamic Host Configuration Protocol (DHCP) are network services that play foundational roles in ensuring smooth and efficient functionality of both local networks and the Internet.

Understanding DNS: DNS is essentially the phone book of the Internet. It translates user-friendly domain names, like www.example.com, into numerical IP addresses, like 192.168.1.1, necessary for locating and identifying computer services with underlying network protocols. When a URL is entered into a browser, it triggers a DNS query. This query cascades through a series of DNS servers, from local to possibly authoritative servers for the domain, to retrieve the appropriate IP address, allowing web resources to be accessed by name rather than by a complex numerical code.

Understanding DHCP: DHCP streamlines network management by automatically assigning IP addresses and other critical network settings to devices joining a network. It operates on a client-server model; when a device connects to the network, it sends out a broadcast request for an IP address. A DHCP server responds with an IP address offer, and upon the client's acceptance, the server finalizes the IP address assignment. This automation greatly reduces the need for manual network configuration, minimizes errors, and lessens administrative overhead.

Integration and Importance of DNS and DHCP: DNS and DHCP often operate in tandem to facilitate seamless network connectivity. This integration allows devices to automatically receive both an IP address and the necessary DNS settings, ensuring efficient network connections, particularly in dynamic environments where devices frequently connect and disconnect.

Security Considerations: Both DNS and DHCP are susceptible to specific types of attacks which can compromise network security. DNS attacks, such as spoofing or cache poisoning, can misdirect users to malicious sites. Similarly, DHCP-related security issues might involve rogue DHCP servers distributing incorrect network configuration data. To mitigate these risks, security protocols such as DNSSEC (DNS Security Extensions) for DNS and DHCP snooping for DHCP are crucial, enhancing the integrity and trustworthiness of these essential services.

6.2 Key Services: Email, FTP, and Web

Email: Email allows for the sending and receiving of messages and digital files across a network using protocols like SMTP for dispatching emails, and POP or IMAP for retrieving them from the server. This service simplifies communication, making it possible to exchange a wide range of information quickly and efficiently across great distances.

File Transfer Protocol (FTP): FTP is crucial for transferring files between networked computers, allowing for file uploads, downloads, and management on a server. This protocol is vital for handling large files or managing files across different locations, providing options for both anonymous and authenticated sessions to cater to various security needs.

Web Services: Web services facilitate machine-to-machine interactions over networks using standards such as HTTP, XML, SOAP, and REST. These services are fundamental to modern web applications, supporting activities from online shopping to social media interactions. They allow for the seamless exchange of data between disparate systems, enhancing functionality and user experience across the internet.

Security and Management: Maintaining security for these services involves implementing specific measures tailored to each service—using enhanced security protocols for email, employing secure methods for FTP transfers like FTPS or SFTP, and ensuring web services communicate over secure HTTPS connections. Regularly managing these services requires monitoring their performance, updating software and protocols as necessary, and adhering to configuration best practices to ensure optimal functionality and security.

6.3 Remote Access Services Overview

Remote access services are essential for businesses that support flexible work arrangements, allowing employees and administrators to connect to networks or computers from remote locations effectively.

Virtual Private Network (VPN): VPNs secure and encrypt connections over less secure networks like the internet, creating a protected "tunnel" for data. This makes VPNs crucial for remote workers who need to access sensitive company resources securely. They can be set up using various protocols such as PPTP, L2TP, OpenVPN, and IPsec, each providing different security levels and compatibility depending on the organizational needs. VPNs are particularly important for safeguarding data integrity and confidentiality when accessing networks from public or insecure Wi-Fi.

Remote Desktop Services (RDS): RDS enables users to control a remote computer or virtual machine over a network. This service is widely used for system maintenance, supporting remote employees, and accessing workplace environments from personal devices. Technologies like Microsoft Remote Desktop, Citrix, or VNC are commonly used to facilitate these connections, offering tools necessary for effective remote desktop management. RDS is essential for enabling real-time collaboration and troubleshooting, allowing applications to run on corporate networks from anywhere.

Direct Access: Direct Access provides an automatic and persistent connection to an internal network over the internet, offering a seamless connection experience without the need for manual user intervention to start the connection. This is set up mainly on enterprise versions of Windows and is beneficial for organizations that require reliable, constant connectivity for their remote staff, providing a more consistent connection than VPNs.

Security Considerations: Securing remote access involves strong authentication methods like two-factor authentication to ensure that only authorized users can access the network. High-level encryption is crucial to protect the data transmitted during remote sessions from potential interception. Additionally, continuous monitoring of remote access activities is vital for detecting and responding to security threats promptly.

Best Practices: Developing comprehensive policies that clearly define remote access permissions, regular updates, and patch management are crucial to maintaining the security integrity of remote access setups.

Additionally, training users on secure remote access practices is fundamental to mitigating risks associated with remote networking.

6.4 Managing Directory Services

Directory services are integral to network management, functioning as centralized hubs for organizing and accessing data related to network resources, such as user accounts and system settings. Here's how directory services are managed effectively:

Overview and Functionality: Directory services like Microsoft Active Directory, LDAP (Lightweight Directory Access Protocol), and Novell eDirectory help network administrators manage users, groups, permissions, and other network-related data. Their primary role is to centralize network management, enforce security policies, and simplify access to network resources.

Key Components:

- **Directories** store detailed information about users and resources.

- **Domain Controllers** handle security authentication requests within a network domain.

- **Schema** dictates the structure of stored data, defining object classes and attributes within the directory.

Implementation Considerations: Effective directory services require scalability planning to accommodate user growth and resource demands. In larger networks, replicating directory information across multiple servers can ensure data accessibility and system resilience, aiding in load balancing and fault tolerance.

Security Management: Security is paramount in directory services. Implementing robust access controls helps ensure that users can only access resources appropriate to their roles. Regular security audits can help maintain compliance with security policies and identify potential vulnerabilities.

Integration with Other Services: Directory services often integrate with other network services like email, collaboration tools, DHCP, DNS, and authentication systems to streamline network management and maintain consistency across various services.

Maintenance and Troubleshooting: Proactive monitoring of directory services is essential for maintaining system health and performance. Regular backups and well-planned recovery procedures are critical for restoring services quickly in case of a system failure.

Best Practices: Keeping directory service software updated is crucial for security. Training IT staff in the management and troubleshooting of directory services ensures they are prepared to handle issues efficiently.

6.5 The Role of Cloud Services

Cloud services have become integral to modern business operations, offering a range of scalable, internet-based resources that significantly boost network efficiency and capabilities. These services cater to various needs, encompassing Software as a Service (SaaS) and Infrastructure as a Service (IaaS), among others. Each type of service provides distinct advantages, making them essential for diverse applications in today's digitally connected world.

Types of Cloud Services:

- **Software as a Service (SaaS):** This model offers applications over the internet on a subscription basis, eliminating the need for internal infrastructure or IT staff. Common SaaS examples include email platforms like Gmail and productivity tools like Microsoft 365.

- **Platform as a Service (PaaS):** PaaS provides a framework for developers to build upon, helping users create applications without managing underlying infrastructure. Platforms like Google App Engine serve as prime examples.

- **Infrastructure as a Service (IaaS):** IaaS supplies essential computing resources, such as virtual servers and storage over the internet, with services like AWS and Microsoft Azure leading the market.

Benefits of Cloud Services:

- **Accessibility:** Facilitates easy access to data and applications from anywhere, supporting remote work and broad operational needs.

- **Disaster Recovery:** Offers robust backup solutions, ensuring business continuity with minimal downtime.

- **Cost Efficiency:** Reduces the capital expenditure of hardware and diminishes maintenance costs.

Integration and Management:

- **Seamless Integration:** Allows for the creation of hybrid environments that combine on-premises infrastructure with cloud resources, optimizing performance and security.

- **Centralized Management:** Cloud providers offer tools that help businesses monitor and manage their cloud infrastructure efficiently.

Security Considerations:

- **Data Security:** Despite advanced security measures provided by cloud services, organizations must take proactive steps to secure their data, including encryption and rigorous access controls.

- **Compliance:** Ensures that cloud deployments adhere to relevant laws and regulations, critical for businesses in regulated industries.

Future Trends:

- **Multi-Cloud Strategies:** Increasingly, companies are using multiple cloud providers to enhance service reliability and security.

- **Edge Computing:** Combining cloud services with edge computing reduces latency, processing data closer to its source, ideal for time-sensitive applications.

Cloud services are transforming how businesses operate, offering flexible, cost-effective solutions that support widespread digital transformation.

6.6 Monitoring and Managing Network Services

Monitoring and managing network services effectively involves a variety of tools and strategies that help maintain the health and efficiency of network infrastructures.

Monitoring Tools and Techniques: Tools like Nagios, Zabbix, and SolarWinds play a pivotal role in overseeing network operations. They provide detailed insights into network traffic, device performance, and system health, and alert administrators to issues such as congestion or unauthorized access attempts. Regularly tracking performance metrics like bandwidth usage and packet loss is vital for identifying and resolving network issues promptly.

Configuration Management: Automated configuration tools such as Ansible, Chef, and Puppet enhance network management by streamlining configuration tasks. This automation helps minimize human errors and maintain uniform settings across the network's devices. Conducting routine configuration audits ensures that network setups adhere to required standards and guidelines, aiding in maintaining system integrity and security.

Security Management: Deploying security systems like Intrusion Detection and Prevention Systems (IDS/IPS) and robust firewalls is fundamental to protecting network data. These systems monitor network traffic continuously and can autonomously respond to suspicious activities, helping safeguard against potential threats.

Quality of Service (QoS) Management: Implementing QoS settings helps prioritize important network traffic, ensuring that critical applications, such as real-time communication tools, operate efficiently even during peak usage. Enforcing QoS policies effectively manages resource allocation, enhancing overall network performance.

Incident Response and Troubleshooting: Establishing a proactive incident response strategy allows for quick reaction to network issues, reducing downtime and mitigating potential impacts. Performing comprehensive root cause analysis helps in identifying the underlying causes of issues, preventing their recurrence.

Reporting and Analytics: Generating regular reports on performance and security helps stakeholders understand the operational status of network services and informs strategic decision-making. Utilizing advanced analytics can also predict potential problems before they affect users, allowing for preemptive action.

Integration with Cloud Services: In environments that integrate both on-premises and cloud-based services, ensuring cohesive monitoring across all platforms is key. This helps maintain a consistent overview of the network's health and performance.

Through these practices, networks can achieve high levels of reliability and performance, adapting to the complexities of modern digital environments.

Chapter 7: Wireless Network Operations

7.1 Wireless Networking Basics

Wireless networking facilitates the connection and communication of devices without the need for physical cables. It uses radio waves or infrared signals to transmit data, providing the flexibility and mobility that wired networks lack. Here are some key elements and concepts that define wireless networking:

Wireless Standards: The IEEE 802.11 family comprises several standards that govern wireless local area network (WLAN) communications, including different specifications for frequency, range, and data transmission rates. These standards have evolved over time, from 802.11a through 802.11ax (Wi-Fi 6), with each iteration improving on speed, efficiency, and range.

Frequency Bands: Wireless networks primarily operate across two frequency bands: 2.4 GHz and 5 GHz. The 2.4 GHz band, while offering a broader range, is more prone to interference from household electronics like microwaves and Bluetooth devices. In contrast, the 5 GHz band provides faster data transmission speeds and suffers less interference but has a reduced range.

Key Components:

- **Wireless Router:** This device connects the local network to the internet, directing data flow between devices on the network and managing traffic.

- **Access Points (APs):** These are used to extend the range of the wireless network, rebroadcasting signals from the router to cover larger areas and accommodate more devices.

- **Wireless Network Interface Cards (NICs):** These enable devices such as smartphones, laptops, and tablets to connect to a wireless network.

Network Topologies:

- **Ad-Hoc Network:** In this setup, devices connect directly to each other without a central device. It's ideal for small, temporary networks where simplicity is key.

- **Infrastructure Network:** More common in home and business environments, this topology involves devices connecting through a central router or access point, allowing for greater scalability.

Wireless Protocols:

- **Wi-Fi Protected Access (WPA/WPA2/WPA3):** These are security protocols that help secure wireless networks. WPA2 is widely used for its robust security features, while WPA3 is the latest standard offering even stronger security.

- **Bluetooth:** Enables short-range data exchange between devices like phones, computers, and peripherals.

- **Zigbee and Z-Wave:** These protocols are typically used in home automation, connecting low-power devices within the home.

Signal Range and Strength: The range of a wireless network is influenced by the power of the transmitter, the sensitivity of the receiver, and external factors such as physical obstructions and interference from other devices. The choice of wireless standard also plays a critical role in the overall signal quality and network performance.

7.2 How to Set Up a Wireless Network

Setting up a wireless network involves a series of important steps to ensure optimal performance and security. Here's a step-by-step guide to creating a functional and secure wireless environment:

Selecting the Right Equipment:

- **Wireless Router:** Choose a router that supports current Wi-Fi standards like Wi-Fi 5 or Wi-Fi 6 to ensure compatibility and future-proofing. Make sure it can adequately cover the size of your area.

- **Access Points (APs):** For extending coverage in large spaces or across multiple rooms, consider deploying additional access points.

Planning Your Network Layout:

- **Site Survey:** Conduct an assessment of your site to find optimal locations for your router and access points, considering how walls, furniture, and other obstructions might affect signal strength.

- **Coverage Area:** Position your equipment to minimize dead zones, ensuring comprehensive coverage throughout the intended area.

Configuring the Wireless Router:

- **Connection:** Initially connect to your router with a wired connection or use the default wireless network details provided with the device.

- **Interface Access:** Log into the router's configuration page using its IP address found in the manual.

- **Network Settings:** Update the network name (SSID) and set a strong password to secure your network.

Securing the Wireless Network:

- **Encryption:** Enable WPA2 or WPA3 encryption to secure your network communications.

- **Admin Access:** Change the default admin username and password to prevent unauthorized adjustments to your settings.

- **WPS Settings:** Disable Wi-Fi Protected Setup if not required, as it can be a potential security risk.

Optimizing Network Settings:

- **Channel Selection:** Use a tool like Wi-Fi Analyzer to choose a less congested wireless channel for better performance.

- **Compatibility Mode:** Ensure the network mode accommodates all your devices, adjusting settings to include older technology if necessary.

Connecting Devices and Testing:

- **Device Setup:** Connect each device by selecting your network's SSID and entering the password.

- **Performance Checks:** Test the connection stability across various devices and locations within your network to ensure consistent accessibility.

Troubleshooting and Maintenance:

- **Problem Solving:** If connectivity problems or dead zones occur, reevaluate the placement of your router or the need for additional access points.

- **Firmware and Monitoring:** Regularly update your router's firmware and monitor network performance to maintain security and efficiency.

7.3 Securing Wireless Networks

Securing your wireless network is vital to prevent unauthorized access and protect sensitive information. Here are several strategies to enhance the security of your wireless setup:

Use Strong Encryption:

- **Latest Encryption Standards:** Opt for WPA3 encryption to ensure the highest level of security. If your devices do not all support WPA3, use WPA2 with a complex passphrase.

Change Default Settings:

- **Router Credentials:** Replace the default administrative credentials with a unique username and strong password to limit unauthorized access.

- **Network Name:** Customize the default SSID to something unique that doesn't reveal personal or organizational details.

Disable Unused Features:

- **Wi-Fi Protected Setup (WPS):** Turn off WPS to close security gaps it might present.

- **Remote Management:** Disable remote management to prevent external access to your router's settings.

Enable Network Filtering:

- **MAC Address Filtering:** Use MAC address filtering to allow only recognized devices to connect to your network, adding an extra layer of control.

Limit Wireless Signal Range:

- **Adjust Router Power:** If your router settings allow, reduce the signal range to limit how far your network extends beyond your immediate area.

Secure Physical Access:

- **Router Security:** Ensure your router is physically secure to prevent unauthorized physical interactions.

Keep Firmware Updated:

- **Firmware Updates:** Regularly update your router's firmware to benefit from the latest security patches and enhancements.

Monitor Network Activity:

- **Network Monitoring:** Utilize tools to monitor who connects to your network and manage network activities. Alert signs like unknown devices or high data usage might indicate security breaches.

Implement a Guest Network:

- **Separate Access:** Use a guest network for visitors, which helps protect your main network's integrity by isolating guest traffic from your primary network.

Use VPNs for Enhanced Security:

- **VPN Usage:** Employ VPNs to encrypt data traffic, particularly beneficial when accessing the network remotely or dealing with sensitive information.

7.4 Future Wireless Technologies

The landscape of wireless technology is rapidly advancing, introducing new technologies that are set to redefine connectivity and enhance how we interact with the digital world.

5G and Beyond:

- **Enhanced Capabilities:** 5G technology promises transformative changes with drastically increased speeds, reduced latency, and greater capacity than 4G. These improvements will support more powerful mobile broadband experiences and enable technologies like virtual reality (VR), augmented reality (AR), and seamless video streaming.

- **IoT Integration:** The integration capabilities of 5G will significantly boost the Internet of Things (IoT), enabling massive device connectivity that will drive advancements in smart cities, automated industries, and intelligent transport systems.

Wi-Fi 6 and Wi-Fi 6E:

- **Efficiency and Performance:** Wi-Fi 6 enhances network efficiency with better throughput, especially in crowded areas, and improved latency and power efficiency for devices.

- **Expanded Spectrum with Wi-Fi 6E:** Wi-Fi 6E extends into the 6 GHz band, offering additional bandwidth and channels to alleviate congestion, providing a boon for high-density environments and applications requiring high data transfer rates.

Terahertz (THz) Wireless Communications:

- **Ultra-High-Frequency Potential:** Terahertz wireless explores frequencies above 100 GHz to 10 THz, aiming to support data rates in the gigabits or even terabits per second, which could revolutionize ultra-fast wireless communications.

- **Emerging Applications:** Although facing challenges like signal attenuation, potential applications for terahertz technology include ultra-fast internet services and rapid large-scale data transfers.

Li-Fi (Light Fidelity):

- **Optical Data Transmission:** Li-Fi technology uses light to transmit data, offering advantages such as faster speeds and enhanced security, as the signal is contained within light-visible environments and cannot penetrate opaque surfaces.

- **Specialized Applications:** Li-Fi is especially promising in environments where radio frequency signals pose a risk or are ineffective, such as in hospitals, on aircraft, or in industrial settings.

Integrated Satellite and Terrestrial Networks:

- **Expanding Global Connectivity:** Integrating satellite communications with terrestrial networks aims to extend reliable connectivity to the most remote areas, supporting global internet access and enhancing communication during disaster recovery scenarios.

- **Technology Convergence:** This integration is a convergence of different communication technologies, ensuring continuous global connectivity and network resilience.

Advanced Network Security Technologies:

- **Robust Security Measures:** As network speeds and accessibility increase, security technologies must evolve to offer stronger encryption and more dynamic authentication methods, safeguarding against sophisticated cyber threats.

AI-Driven Network Management:

- **Smart Network Operations:** Artificial intelligence and machine learning are set to transform network management by optimizing network performance and security dynamically, predicting network loads, and detecting and responding to anomalies in real-time.

7.5 Troubleshooting Wireless Issues

While wireless networks offer great flexibility and convenience, they can sometimes encounter performance issues that disrupt connectivity and data transmission. Here's a guide to understanding common wireless problems and how to troubleshoot them effectively:

1. Connectivity Problems:

- **Symptoms:** Difficulty connecting to the network, frequent disconnections, or no internet access.

- **Troubleshooting Steps:**

    - Ensure that the router or access point is powered on with LEDs indicating normal operations.

    - Check that the device is within the signal range and not obstructed by physical barriers like walls.

    - Confirm the network SSID and password are entered correctly.

    - Restart the router to reset the network connection.

2. Slow Wireless Speeds:

- **Symptoms:** Decreased internet speed, delays in file transfers, or streaming video buffers.

- **Troubleshooting Steps:**

    - Test the connection on various devices to see if the problem is isolated.

    - Switch the router's Wi-Fi channel to reduce interference from other networks.

    - Update the router's firmware to enhance performance.

    - Limit the number of active devices to alleviate network congestion.

3. Poor Signal Strength:

- **Symptoms:** Weak signal indicated on devices, particularly far from the router.

- **Troubleshooting Steps:**

    - Move the router to a more central location to enhance coverage.

    - Keep the router away from other electronic devices that could interfere with the signal.

    - Install a Wi-Fi repeater or extender to boost the signal reach.

4. Frequent Disconnections:

- **Symptoms:** Devices regularly losing connection to the network.

- **Troubleshooting Steps:**

    - Update wireless adapter drivers and router firmware.

    - Change to a less congested Wi-Fi channel.

    - Review and adjust router security settings if they are too restrictive.

5. Network Security Issues:

- **Symptoms:** Unrecognized devices on the network or potential security breaches.

- **Troubleshooting Steps:**

    - Update the network's SSID and password to more secure options.

    - Enable WPA2 or WPA3 encryption.

    - Regularly monitor connected devices and block any unfamiliar ones.

6. Device-Specific Issues:

- **Symptoms:** A single device is unable to connect, while others connect normally.

- **Troubleshooting Steps:**

    - Ensure the device's network drivers and operating system are up to date.

    - Forget and reconnect to the Wi-Fi network on the device.

    - Check for any apps or settings, such as VPNs or security software, that might interfere with connectivity.

7.6 Best Practices for Wireless Management

Managing a wireless network effectively goes beyond the initial setup; it encompasses continuous monitoring, strategic updates, and adherence to best practices to maintain optimal functionality, security, and scalability. Here are key strategies to ensure your wireless network remains robust and secure:

Regular Firmware and Software Updates: Keep your network devices, such as routers and access points, updated with the latest firmware and software to address vulnerabilities, enhance security, and improve stability and performance.

Optimize Equipment Placement: Strategically place your routers and access points to maximize coverage and minimize interference. They should be central, elevated, and clear of physical and electronic interference from items like microwaves and cordless phones.

Secure Wireless Access: Implement the highest level of encryption available (preferably WPA2 or WPA3) to protect against unauthorized access. Change default passwords and network names (SSIDs) to complex, unique alternatives. Consider setting up a separate network for guests to enhance security.

Implement Strong Authentication Measures: Employ robust authentication methods, such as multi-factor authentication, for network access, especially for administrative tasks. For larger networks, consider using protocols like RADIUS for more effective user access management.

Monitor and Analyze Network Performance: Utilize tools like Wireshark or SolarWinds to monitor network performance, identify bandwidth issues, or detect interference. Regularly conduct wireless site surveys to adjust the setup or configuration, ensuring optimal performance.

Manage Bandwidth Usage: Use Quality of Service (QoS) settings to prioritize bandwidth for critical applications, such as VoIP and video conferencing. Restrict bandwidth for non-essential applications to maintain performance levels across the network.

Plan for Scalability: Design your network to easily accommodate growth in the number of devices and data traffic. This foresight will help in maintaining performance levels without costly and time-consuming overhauls.

Educate Users: Inform network users about secure practices, such as recognizing security threats like phishing attacks, securing personal devices, and the importance of updates.

Backup Configurations: Regularly back up your network configurations. This ensures that you can quickly restore your network settings after any hardware failure or other disruptions, minimizing downtime.

By implementing these best practices, you can maintain a secure, efficient, and scalable wireless network that adapts to evolving user needs and technological advancements. Regular reviews and updates of these practices are crucial as new technologies and threats emerge.

Chapter 8: Ensuring Network Security

8.1 Introduction to Security in Networking

Network security is a fundamental aspect of managing IT systems, focusing on protecting network integrity, confidentiality, and availability using a combination of hardware and software solutions. Here are the main goals and reasons why network security is indispensable:

Core Objectives of Network Security:

- **Confidentiality:** Ensures that sensitive information is accessible only to authorized users.

- **Integrity:** Maintains the accuracy and completeness of data, safeguarding it from unauthorized changes.

- **Availability:** Keeps network services up and running for users, minimizing disruptions and downtimes.

Importance of Network Security:

- **Protection Against Cyber Threats:** With the escalation of cybercrime, it is crucial to defend networks against diverse threats such as viruses, ransomware, and phishing.

- **Data Security:** Both organizations and individuals depend on digital data which must be shielded from unauthorized access, corruption, or loss.

- **Regulatory Compliance:** Various industries face strict regulations requiring the protection of sensitive data, making network security essential for legal compliance.

- **Trust Building:** Robust network security fosters trust among users and stakeholders by ensuring data safety and network reliability.

Challenges Facing Network Security:

- **Evolving Threat Landscape:** Cyber threats are constantly changing, growing more sophisticated and challenging to detect.

- **Network Complexity:** Modern networks, which often blend wired and wireless components and span multiple devices, can introduce numerous vulnerabilities.

- **Human Factors:** The human element often poses significant security risks. Mistakes such as weak passwords, mishandling of data, and susceptibility to social engineering attacks can undermine network security measures.

8.2 Identifying Threats and Vulnerabilities

Securing a network effectively starts by understanding the various threats and vulnerabilities it might face. Here's an exploration of the common risks and weak points that can impact network security:

Common Network Threats:

- **Malware:** This category includes viruses, worms, Trojans, and ransomware, which can disrupt operations, steal sensitive information, and even cause physical damage to hardware.

- **Phishing Attacks:** These deceptive strategies involve sending fraudulent communications, often via email, that mimic reputable sources to steal sensitive data such as credit card details and login credentials.

- **Denial of Service (DoS) and Distributed Denial of Service (DDoS) Attacks:** These attacks aim to render a network resource unavailable to its intended users by overwhelming it with malicious traffic.

- **Man-in-the-Middle (MitM) Attacks:** In these attacks, the attacker secretly intercepts and may alter communications between two parties who think they are communicating directly.

- **SQL Injection:** This attack involves embedding malicious code into an SQL-using server, enabling the attacker to access and alter the database, which can lead to the theft or loss of data.

Common Network Vulnerabilities:

- **Software Flaws:** Bugs or flaws in software can open doors for unauthorized access or other malicious actions.

- **Weak Network Policies:** Inadequately defined or enforced network policies, such as insufficient password policies and access controls, can make networks vulnerable to attacks.

- **Configuration Errors:** Incorrectly configured firewalls, routers, and switches can leave networks exposed. This can include issues like open ports, unsecured admin interfaces, or improper settings adjustments.

- **Outdated Security Software:** Neglecting to update security software can leave a network defenseless against new types of attacks. Keeping software updated is vital to guarding against recently discovered vulnerabilities.

Methods for Identifying Threats and Vulnerabilities:

- **Risk Assessment:** Conducting regular risk assessments can help pinpoint potential threats to the network and assess their risk level.

- **Penetration Testing:** Utilizing ethical hacking techniques to evaluate the robustness of networks and system defenses.

- **Security Audits:** Periodic reviews by internal or external auditors can help uncover vulnerabilities and ensure compliance with established security policies.

- **Intrusion Detection and Prevention Systems (IDS/IPS):** These tools monitor network traffic for suspicious activities and known threats, providing essential security intelligence.

Staying Ahead of Emerging Threats:

- **Stay Informed:** Keeping up to date with the latest in security news, threat reports, and advisories from trusted sources is crucial.

- **Training and Awareness Programs:** Regular educational programs for employees can help mitigate the risk of security breaches caused by human error, often considered one of the biggest threats to network security.

8.3 Implementing Security Protocols and Measures

To safeguard networks against a range of threats and vulnerabilities, it's critical to implement a set of robust security protocols and measures. These protocols are the backbone of network security, designed to prevent unauthorized access and data breaches. Here's a guide on effectively deploying these security measures within an organization:

Strong Encryption Practices:

- **For Data in Transit:** Use robust encryption protocols such as HTTPS, SSL/TLS, and secure VPNs to protect data as it travels across the network, preventing interception or unauthorized access.

- **For Data at Rest:** Encrypt sensitive data stored on network servers and devices, ensuring its safety even if physical security measures fail.

Authentication and Access Management:

- **Multi-Factor Authentication (MFA):** Implement MFA to add an extra layer of security, requiring users to provide multiple forms of verification before gaining access to network resources.

- **Role-Based Access Control (RBAC):** Use RBAC to limit user access to essential resources based on their roles, minimizing the potential damage from compromised credentials.

Network Segmentation and Isolation:

- **Segmentation:** Break down the network into smaller, manageable and secure segments, reducing the lateral movement of attackers within the network.

- **Isolation:** Separate sensitive network areas from less critical ones, such as isolating critical servers or data stores from general user access areas.

Regular Updates and Patch Management:

- **Patch Management:** Maintain a routine for updating all software and firmware with the latest security patches to protect against known vulnerabilities and exploits.

Firewalls and Intrusion Prevention Systems:

- **Firewalls:** Set up firewalls to create a barrier between your trusted internal network and untrusted external networks, regulating traffic based on predefined security rules.

- **Intrusion Prevention Systems (IPS):** Deploy IPS to actively monitor network traffic for suspicious activity and automatically block potential threats.

Comprehensive Security Policies and Incident Management:

- **Security Policies:** Establish and maintain detailed security policies that address every aspect of network security from user conduct to specific protocols for managing data breaches.

- **Incident Response Plan:** Develop a clear incident response strategy that includes procedures for containment, eradication, recovery, and a thorough analysis after an incident.

Employee Training and Security Awareness:

- **Regular Training:** Provide ongoing education and awareness programs to all employees about potential security threats like phishing and safe practices for using IT resources.

Continuous Monitoring and Proactive Testing:

- **Network Monitoring:** Employ SIEM systems for real-time monitoring and analysis of security alerts generated by network hardware and applications.

- **Penetration Testing:** Schedule regular penetration testing to proactively find and fix vulnerabilities before they can be exploited by external threats.

8.4 Crafting a Security Policy

Creating a comprehensive security policy is crucial for guiding an organization's protective measures against network threats. This policy serves as a foundational document that outlines the responsibilities, procedures, and rules for safeguarding network assets. Here's how to develop an effective security policy:

Establish Scope and Objectives:

- **Scope:** Clearly define what the policy covers, including which parts of the network, which data, and which users are included.

- **Objectives:** Set clear goals for the policy, focusing on ensuring the confidentiality, integrity, and availability of network resources.

Asset and Risk Management:

- **Asset Identification:** Catalog all critical assets that need protection, such as hardware, software, and sensitive data.

- **Risk Assessment:** Perform thorough evaluations to identify potential threats and vulnerabilities, assess their impact, and prioritize them based on their potential damage.

Developing Security Controls:

- **Preventive Measures:** Outline controls designed to prevent incidents, such as deploying firewalls and antivirus systems.

- **Detection Strategies:** Set up systems to detect and alert on security breaches, such as using monitoring tools and managing logs.

- **Corrective Actions:** Plan for responses to security incidents, including data recovery processes and incident response protocols.

Roles and Responsibilities:

- **Define Responsibilities:** Assign specific security responsibilities to personnel, detailing who is responsible for implementing, monitoring, and maintaining security measures.

Detailing Security Procedures:

- **Document Procedures:** Write down step-by-step actions for crucial security processes, including handling user authentication, managing network access, and responding to security incidents.

Compliance:

- **Regulatory Adherence:** Ensure the policy complies with relevant legal and regulatory requirements, which might include GDPR, HIPAA, or PCI-DSS, depending on the organization's location and sector.

Training and Awareness:

- **Ongoing Education:** Develop continuous training programs to educate employees about security practices and potential risks, helping to mitigate breaches caused by human error.

Policy Maintenance:

- **Regular Reviews:** Set a routine for regularly reviewing and updating the policy to adapt to new threats, technological advances, and changes in business strategy.

Enforcement and Accessibility:

- **Enforcement:** Specify the consequences of not adhering to the policy to ensure compliance and discipline.

- **Accessibility:** Ensure that the policy is easily accessible to all employees and stakeholders, and communicate its importance and everyone's role in enforcing it.

8.5 Tools for Enhancing Network Security

Organizations deploy a variety of advanced tools to bolster network security, addressing prevention, detection, and response to diverse and evolving threats. These tools are critical for safeguarding networks from unauthorized access and cyber attacks. Here's a closer look at the essential tools that fortify network defenses:

1. Firewalls: Firewalls serve as the first line of defense, regulating both inbound and outbound network traffic based on predefined security rules. They can be implemented as hardware, software, or a hybrid form, and advanced models known as next-generation firewalls integrate additional features like application awareness.

2. Antivirus and Anti-malware Software: This software is crucial for detecting and neutralizing malware such as viruses, worms, and trojans. It provides real-time scanning capabilities, heuristic analysis to catch new threats, and web protection to prevent access to harmful sites.

3. Intrusion Detection and Prevention Systems (IDPS): These systems monitor network activity to identify and react to suspicious behavior. An intrusion detection system (IDS) sends alerts about potential threats, while an intrusion prevention system (IPS) actively blocks these threats.

4. Security Information and Event Management (SIEM): SIEM technology aggregates and analyzes log data from various sources within the network, providing real-time monitoring and helping to detect and respond to security incidents efficiently.

5. Virtual Private Networks (VPN): VPNs encrypt data transmitted over potentially insecure networks, providing secure remote access to the organizational network, which is especially important for mobile employees or when using public Wi-Fi.

6. Network Access Control (NAC): NAC systems ensure that all devices connected to the network comply with security policies before access is granted. They can restrict access to non-compliant devices and enforce policies based on user roles.

7. Encryption Tools: These tools are essential for protecting sensitive data, ensuring that information at rest and in transit is accessible only to authorized users.

8. Patch Management Software: Keeping software and firmware up to date is crucial to defend against known vulnerabilities. Patch management tools automate the updating process to ensure that all parts of the network are protected against potential exploits.

9. Advanced Threat Protection (ATP): ATP tools utilize a range of techniques, including sandboxing and machine learning, to detect and defend against sophisticated cyber threats that traditional tools might miss.

8.6 Real-World Security Implementation Case Studies

Learning from real-world security implementations provides invaluable insights into effective strategies that various sectors employ to protect their networks and sensitive data. The following case studies showcase how diverse industries tackle their unique security challenges:

Financial Services Sector: A leading bank continually faced phishing threats aimed at their customers' financial data. Their robust approach included educating employees on recognizing phishing schemes, employing advanced email filtering technologies, and enforcing multi-factor authentication for access to banking services. This holistic strategy significantly lowered the incidence of successful phishing attacks, enhancing the bank's security framework.

Healthcare Provider: A healthcare organization required stringent measures to secure patient data while adhering to HIPAA regulations. They implemented a robust VPN with strong encryption, applied role-based access controls, and conducted regular security audits. These measures ensured the safe remote access of sensitive patient data, effectively minimizing the risk of data breaches while maintaining regulatory compliance.

Retail Corporation: A global retail chain addressing recurrent data breaches involving credit card information chose to upgrade its payment systems. By integrating end-to-end encryption and tokenization of credit card details, and segmenting the payment systems away from other network areas, the retailer significantly reduced credit card fraud and restored consumer trust.

Government Agency: Facing potential cyber-espionage, a government agency fortified its communication and data storage systems. They adopted extensive encryption across all communication channels and storage systems, utilized sophisticated intrusion detection systems, and regularly trained staff on security protocols. These proactive measures drastically reduced espionage risks and unauthorized data access, safeguarding sensitive governmental information.

Technology Startup: A rapidly expanding tech startup with a primarily remote workforce needed a scalable security solution to protect intellectual property while fostering collaboration. Opting for a cloud-based security service, they managed to secure cloud storage, integrate real-time threat detection, and automate security updates, thereby supporting their growth and innovative processes without heavy initial investment in physical security infrastructure.

Each case illustrates that tailored security strategies, integrating advanced technology, stringent policies, and continual training, are crucial for effectively safeguarding networks and sensitive data across various sectors. These examples emphasize the importance of adapting security measures to meet specific industry risks and compliance needs while employing both traditional and cutting-edge technologies to strengthen security resilience.

Chapter 9: Network Management Techniques

9.1 Basics of Network Management

Network management is a comprehensive discipline that involves various strategies and techniques essential for maintaining, operating, and administering a computer network. It is aimed at ensuring that the network operates smoothly and efficiently while being secure and reliable. Here's an exploration of the fundamental aspects involved in effective network management:

Network Planning and Design: This foundational stage involves thoroughly understanding the intended scale, purpose, and specific requirements of the network. Effective planning anticipates not only the current needs but also future expansion and scaling. Design choices then follow, focusing on selecting the right network architecture and technologies that align with the organization's operational goals and budget constraints.

Network Deployment: This stage includes the physical and software setup of the network. It covers the installation of critical network infrastructure such as routers, switches, and servers, as well as the configuration of these devices to meet predefined network specifications and policies.

Routine Network Operations: Daily management tasks are crucial for the ongoing health of the network. These include active monitoring of network traffic, adjusting resources as needed, and managing user access and data flow to ensure optimal network performance and efficiency.

Ongoing Maintenance: Proactive maintenance practices are vital. This involves regular updates and patch management to secure and enhance network functionality, as well as swift troubleshooting to resolve issues and minimize downtime.

Network Security Management: Developing robust security policies and implementing necessary security measures protect the network from potential threats. This includes the use of firewalls, antivirus programs, and other security protocols that safeguard the network against unauthorized access and cyber threats.

Performance Monitoring and Optimization: Utilizing advanced monitoring tools helps in tracking the performance of the network. This is crucial for identifying and rectifying performance bottlenecks. Optimization efforts may involve tweaking settings or upgrading hardware to boost the network's overall efficiency.

Documentation and Compliance: Maintaining detailed and up-to-date documentation of all network configurations, changes, and processes is essential for effective management and compliance with regulatory requirements. This documentation aids in troubleshooting and is vital for audits and maintaining standards compliance.

9.2 Tools for Effective Network Management

The effectiveness of network management can greatly benefit from deploying a variety of specialized tools designed to handle everything from monitoring and controlling to optimizing network performance and security.

Network Monitoring Tools:

- **Nagios**: This open-source tool provides extensive monitoring capabilities, alerting network administrators to problems and recoveries in real time, enhancing network reliability.

- **SolarWinds Network Performance Monitor**: Known for its user-friendly interface, this tool helps in fault monitoring and network performance optimization, offering detailed visual insights.

- **Wireshark**: Essential for protocol analysis, this tool captures and inspects the data traveling over the network, invaluable for troubleshooting and ensuring efficient data communications.

Configuration Management Tools:

- **Ansible**: This tool simplifies complex cloud provisioning, application deployment, and configuration management tasks through automation, enhancing operational efficiency.

- **Chef**: It automates infrastructure management across network environments ensuring consistent and reliable configurations.

- **Puppet**: Ideal for managing infrastructure lifecycles, from provisioning to deployment and ongoing management, Puppet automates administrative tasks effectively.

Security Management Tools:

- **Cisco Identity Services Engine (ISE)**: This tool automates and enforces security access to network resources, enhancing the security posture of an organization.

- **Splunk**: Beyond its primary use in log management, Splunk is also effective for network security monitoring, helping detect and respond to potential threats.

Network Traffic Analysis Tools:

- **NetFlow Analyzer**: Uses the NetFlow protocol to monitor network traffic, aiding in identifying traffic patterns and pinpointing sources of congestion.

- **PRTG Network Monitor**: Offers a comprehensive monitoring solution, providing real-time alerts and insights into network health.

Performance Management Tools:

- **Dynatrace**: Uses AI to provide full-stack monitoring, from applications to databases, and automatically pinpoints performance issues.

- **AppDynamics**: Monitors application performance in real time and detects anomalies, supporting complex application environments.

Backup and Disaster Recovery Tools:

- **Veeam**: Delivers cloud-data management capabilities, ensuring reliable backup and rapid recovery across various environments.

- **Acronis True Image**: Known for robust backup features, this tool also provides effective recovery options and supports multiple platforms.

Compliance and Network Testing Tools:

- **Nmap**: An indispensable tool for network discovery and security auditing, it provides valuable insights into network configurations and security profiles.

- **Qualys**: Offers a range of services from cloud security to compliance management, suitable for businesses of all sizes.

These tools are foundational for a robust network management strategy, aiding in the enhancement of network performance, security, and compliance.

9.3 Performance Monitoring Strategies

Maintaining robust network performance is paramount, requiring continuous evaluation and adaptation. Effective performance monitoring strategies not only ensure the network operates smoothly but also preemptively address potential issues. Here are some essential practices for overseeing network performance:

Establishing a Performance Baseline:

- **Creating Reference Points**: Develop a clear understanding of what constitutes normal operations by establishing baseline metrics for bandwidth, latency, packet loss, and throughput. This reference aids in identifying deviations that may signal underlying problems.

- **Strategic Utilization**: Regularly reference this baseline to quickly spot performance dips or anomalies, facilitating faster troubleshooting and resolution.

Real-Time Monitoring and Alerts:

- **Immediate Insight**: Implement tools that monitor network conditions live, allowing for the immediate detection of performance issues, which is crucial for quick responses to prevent disruptions.

- **Proactive Notifications**: Set up alerts to notify administrators when performance metrics deviate from the norm, ensuring issues can be addressed before they impact users.

Comprehensive Reporting:

- **Routine Analysis**: Automate the generation of detailed reports on a regular basis to track network health, which helps in long-term planning and immediate issue recognition.

- **On-Demand Reporting**: Enable capabilities to create ad-hoc reports for in-depth investigation of specific or unusual network activity.

Advanced Analytics:

- **Trend Examination**: Use advanced tools to analyze long-term performance data to forecast potential future problems, optimize operations, and inform capacity planning.

- **Focused Diagnostics**: Employ diagnostic tools to delve deeply into performance issues, helping to identify specific bottlenecks or points of failure.

Synthetic Traffic Simulation:

- **Predictive Testing**: Employ synthetic monitoring to simulate specific traffic scenarios on the network. This approach is invaluable for stress testing and understanding the impact of network changes on performance before they go live.

End-to-End Performance Testing:

- **Holistic Assessments**: Regularly test network performance from various network points to ensure that all parts of the network integrate seamlessly and meet expected performance standards.

- **User Experience Focus**: Incorporate monitoring that specifically assesses the impact of network performance on end-user satisfaction, as user feedback is vital for assessing the practical impact of network conditions.

Segmented Performance Management:

- **Traffic Isolation**: Strategically segment the network to confine and resolve performance issues within specific areas, preventing widespread impact and enhancing overall network efficiency.

Integrated Incident Management:

- **Seamless Coordination**: Ensure that performance monitoring tools are fully integrated with incident management processes to facilitate swift and effective resolution of performance issues.

9.4 Managing Network Configurations

Overseeing and adapting network configurations is crucial for maintaining a network's reliability, security, and compliance. Here's how to effectively manage these configurations:

Establish Configuration Standards:

- Develop and document standard practices for configuring network devices like routers, switches, and firewalls. This ensures that setups align with industry standards and regulatory requirements.

- Keep a thorough record of all network configuration changes, detailing the reasons for adjustments and any deviations from established standards.

Utilize Automated Tools for Configuration:

- Implement tools like Ansible, Chef, or Puppet for configuration management. These automate the deployment of standardized settings, streamline updates, and support quick rollbacks if issues arise.

- Automation promotes consistency and efficiency, especially across extensive networks or multiple devices.

Implement Version Control:

- Use version control systems to manage changes to configuration files, allowing for tracking adjustments, who made them, and their impact on the network.

- Regularly back up configuration files to enable swift restoration to a functional state if updates cause problems.

Conduct Configuration Audits:

- Regularly review configurations to ensure they comply with both internal policies and external regulations and to identify any incorrect configurations.

- Verify that security configurations, like firewall settings and access controls, are correct and that no vulnerabilities are present.

Manage Changes Carefully:

- Introduce a formal process for making changes to network configurations, including necessary reviews and approvals.

- Analyze the potential impacts of proposed changes to minimize disruptions and unintended effects on network operations.

Train and Educate Staff:

- Ensure that IT staff are well-trained in your organization's configuration management practices and tools.

- Continuously update training materials to reflect new technologies and insights gained from previous experiences.

Integrate with Other IT Management Processes:

- Ensure configuration management is part of a broader IT management strategy that includes performance monitoring, incident management, and security operations. This integration helps create a cohesive management strategy that enhances overall network health.

Focus on Continuous Improvement:

- Set up a feedback system to monitor the effects of configuration changes and learn from these experiences to refine future practices.

9.5 Handling Network Faults

Handling network faults effectively is vital for ensuring the smooth operation of network services. Here are some strategies for managing network faults:

1. Fault Detection:

- **Monitoring Tools**: Employ advanced monitoring tools that provide real-time alerts to detect anomalies or faults in the network.
- **Log Analysis**: Use systems to analyze logs from network devices, aiding in pinpointing faults.

2. Fault Diagnosis:

- **Automated Diagnostics**: Use tools that automatically assess network health and diagnose issues, which might include traffic analysis and device status checks.
- **Root Cause Analysis**: Investigate the underlying causes of faults through a detailed examination of network configurations, hardware, and external impacts.

3. Fault Resolution:

- **Standard Operating Procedures (SOPs)**: Develop SOPs to address common faults efficiently and consistently.
- **Escalation Protocols**: Define clear escalation paths for varying fault severities, ensuring appropriate responses are triggered.

4. Preventive Measures:

- **Proactive Maintenance**: Perform regular maintenance on network components to prevent faults, including firmware updates and hardware inspections.
- **Capacity Planning**: Monitor and adjust network capacity based on usage trends to avoid overloads and ensure reliability.

5. Training and Documentation:

- **Training Programs**: Regularly train network staff on fault management to ensure readiness and familiarity with response procedures.
- **Documentation**: Maintain comprehensive records of faults and their resolutions to help identify trends and inform future prevention strategies.

6. Communication:

- **Internal Communication**: Keep stakeholders informed during major network issues to manage expectations and coordinate responses effectively.
- **Customer Communication**: Communicate openly with customers affected by network issues to maintain trust and manage service expectations.

7. Review and Learn:

- **Post-Mortem Analysis**: After addressing a fault, analyze it to learn from the incident and refine future responses.
- **Continuous Improvement**: Regularly update fault management practices based on new insights and technological advancements.

9.6 Reporting and Analytics in Network Management

Effective network management heavily depends on robust reporting and analytics to offer deep insights into network operations. Here's a detailed look at how these elements are integrated into network management:

1. Data Collection:

- **Sources**: Data is gathered from a wide range of network components like routers, switches, and servers, encompassing traffic data, device statuses, and security logs.

- **Tools**: Advanced network monitoring tools and management software play a key role in aggregating and organizing this data effectively.

2. Real-Time Analytics:

- **Monitoring**: Implement real-time analytics to continuously observe network health, enabling quick identification of issues as they arise.

- **Dashboards**: Use interactive dashboards for a dynamic overview of network status, vital for immediate response and ongoing network operations.

3. Historical Reporting:

- **Trend Analysis**: Historical data analysis helps in recognizing patterns and trends which aid in network capacity planning and anticipating future requirements.

- **Custom Reports**: Tailor reports to focus on specific network areas such as peak usage times or frequent security challenges.

4. Predictive Analytics:

- **Forecasting**: Leverage predictive models to anticipate future network demands based on historical trends, guiding proactive network enhancements.

- **Modeling**: Create simulations of various network scenarios to predict impacts of potential changes and help in decision-making for network upgrades.

5. Diagnostic Analytics:

- **Problem Solving**: When issues arise, diagnostic analytics help delve deeper into the cause, analyzing data to uncover underlying problems.

- **Feedback Loops**: Utilize insights from analytics to refine and improve network monitoring and management practices continuously.

6. Compliance and Security Reporting:

- **Regulatory Compliance**: Ensure the network complies with legal and regulatory standards by regularly generating compliance reports.

- **Security Posture**: Employ analytics to strengthen network security through identification of vulnerabilities and monitoring unusual activities indicating potential security threats.

7. Performance Benchmarks:

- **Benchmarking**: Assess network performance against benchmarks or industry standards to evaluate efficiency and identify areas for improvement.

- **Best Practices**: Update benchmarks over time to keep pace with best practices and advances in technology, enhancing network performance.

8. Integration with Business Intelligence:

- **Business Decisions**: Integrate network analytics with broader business intelligence tools to inform strategic decisions and enhance business operations.

- **Cross-Functional Insights**: Share network performance data across departments to foster a better understanding and collaboration on technology-driven business initiatives.

Chapter 10: Cutting-Edge Network Technologies

10.1 Networking and the IoT Impact

The Internet of Things (IoT) is reshaping the landscape of networking, connecting billions of devices across various sectors, including home automation, industrial applications, healthcare, and smart city projects. This expansion introduces significant changes to network design, demanding increased complexity, heightened security measures, and enhanced connectivity.

Expanding Network Complexity:

- **Device Diversity**: IoT introduces a variety of devices to networks, each with different communication needs and protocols, significantly broadening the types of data handled.

- **Scalability Challenges**: The networks are adapting to manage the sheer volume of IoT devices, which can be in the tens of thousands, all requiring immediate data processing and connectivity.

Elevated Connectivity Requirements:

- **Uninterrupted Connectivity**: Critical applications, like those in healthcare and manufacturing, depend on reliable, continuous connectivity, which compels networks to evolve into more resilient and fault-tolerant systems.

- **Edge Computing**: To effectively manage the massive data generated by IoT devices, networks are integrating more edge computing solutions, allowing data processing closer to the source and reducing latency.

Security and Privacy Enhancements:

- **Broadened Attack Surface**: Each IoT device potentially opens up new vectors for security threats, making robust security protocols essential.

- **Data Privacy Concerns**: With IoT devices frequently collecting personal data, ensuring privacy and adherence to regulations like GDPR is increasingly vital.

Adaptations in Network Infrastructure:

- **Low-Power Network Solutions**: IoT devices, especially in remote deployments, require networks like LPWAN that minimize power consumption and extend device life.

- **5G Technology**: Essential for IoT's expansion, 5G networks provide the necessary speed, capacity, and responsiveness to enable efficient and effective IoT operations.

Development of New Networking Protocols:

- **IoT-Specific Protocols**: Protocols such as MQTT and CoAP are tailored for IoT, optimizing the performance of devices with low bandwidth and power availability.

Revised Network Management Approaches:

- **Automated Systems**: The vast scale of IoT implementations necessitates more sophisticated network management systems, utilizing AI and machine learning to handle network optimization and security proactively.

Business Implications:

- **Emerging Business Models**: IoT enables innovative business models and revenue opportunities, from predictive maintenance to usage-based pricing.

- **Enhanced Operational Efficiency**: IoT offers detailed data insights, helping businesses optimize operations, reduce costs, and enhance service delivery.

The transformation brought about by IoT pushes for networks that are not only more capable and intelligent but also more integral to the operations and strategies of businesses across various industries.

10.2 Blockchain's Role in Networking

Blockchain technology, initially developed for digital currency transactions such as Bitcoin, is now finding innovative uses in networking. This integration promises to revolutionize network management by enhancing security, promoting decentralization, and increasing transparency.

Security Enhancements:

- **Immutable Records**: Blockchain's core feature of providing a tamper-proof ledger ensures that once data is entered, it cannot be altered without network consensus. This characteristic is crucial for securing transactions and data exchanges across networks.

- **Fraud and Tampering Resistance**: The security protocols inherent in blockchain, like robust encryption and its decentralized nature, are vital for protecting sensitive information, particularly in fields such as finance, healthcare, and government.

Decentralization of Network Management:

- **Distributed Control**: By distributing network management, blockchain reduces dependency on central points of control, thereby mitigating risks associated with centralized system failures or attacks.

- **Smart Contracts**: Blockchain facilitates the implementation of smart contracts that autonomously execute agreed-upon terms, streamlining processes from access management to resource distribution without human intervention.

Transparency and Trust:

- **Auditable Transactions**: Blockchain's transparent logging of activities enhances auditability and trustworthiness, making it easier for users and stakeholders to verify and trust network activities.

- **Consensus-Based Operations**: The requirement for consensus in blockchain operations fosters a transparent environment where all changes are agreed upon by all parties, enhancing overall network trust.

Integration with IoT:

- **Securing IoT Networks**: In IoT, blockchain can secure device-to-device communication and ensure data integrity by maintaining a reliable and immutable record of all interactions.

- **Autonomous Device Operations**: Blockchain can enable IoT devices to operate autonomously and securely without the need for centralized control, enhancing efficiency and reliability.

Support for Advanced Network Technologies:

- **Network Slicing and 5G**: In the realm of 5G, blockchain can significantly contribute to network slicing, managing and securing virtual network segments independently on shared physical infrastructures.

Challenges:

- **Scalability Issues**: Blockchain faces scalability challenges, especially as the number of nodes increases, potentially slowing down the processing times.

- **Implementation Complexity**: The adoption of blockchain can introduce significant complexity and overhead costs, requiring careful consideration and management.

10.3 Automating Networks with AI and ML

Artificial Intelligence (AI) and Machine Learning (ML) are revolutionizing network management by automating operations and improving decision-making through advanced analytics. Here's a look at how these technologies are being applied to enhance network functions:

Predictive Maintenance and Traffic Management:

- AI and ML are utilized to analyze traffic patterns and predict future network demands. This foresight aids in proactive network maintenance and capacity planning, ensuring networks are prepared for varying load levels.

- Anomalies in network behavior are quickly identified using ML algorithms, allowing for early detection of potential security risks or performance issues before they escalate.

Automating Network Configurations:

- AI-driven solutions streamline network configuration, significantly reducing manual labor and minimizing human errors. These systems dynamically adjust network settings in real-time based on usage patterns and environmental conditions.

- Networks can autonomously optimize performance, for example, by adjusting traffic routes, managing bandwidth, or balancing loads without human intervention.

Security Enhancements:

- Continuous monitoring of network activities through AI helps to detect unusual behaviors or patterns that may signify potential threats, enabling immediate automated actions to mitigate risks.

- AI also plays a crucial role in managing and updating security policies dynamically, adapting to new threats as they emerge and adjusting network defenses accordingly.

Improving Service Quality:

- AI tools are employed to monitor service quality, ensuring that network adjustments are made in real time to align with service level agreements (SLAs) and enhance user experience.

- Troubleshooting becomes more efficient as AI systems use historical data and performance trends to diagnose issues and suggest optimal solutions, reducing downtime and enhancing service reliability.

Supporting Advanced Network Technologies:

- In 5G networks, AI facilitates the management of network slices, automating the allocation and optimization of resources tailored to specific traffic types and user demands.

- The proliferation of IoT devices and the expansion of edge computing create complex, expansive networks that benefit from AI and ML for efficient data processing and operational automation at the network's edge.

Navigating Challenges:

- The integration of AI in network management introduces complexities and requires skilled professionals to ensure systems operate as intended and make ethically sound decisions.

- As decisions become more automated, maintaining transparency and accountability in AI's actions is essential to ensure trust and reliability in network operations.

The integration of AI and ML into network management signals a shift towards more autonomous, efficient, and secure network operations, paving the way for innovative applications and improved network resilience.

10.4 Understanding Software-Defined Networking (SDN)

Software-Defined Networking (SDN) is revolutionizing traditional network management by offering a more organized, dynamic, and scalable approach. Here's an insight into SDN and its impact on networking:

Core Concepts of SDN:

- **Separation of Control and Data Planes**: SDN divides the networking tasks into two distinct elements: the data plane which handles the physical transmission of data, and the control plane which makes decisions about how traffic is routed. Traditional networks integrate both planes in each network device, but SDN centralizes control functions to enhance efficiency and flexibility.

- **Centralized Management**: With SDN, network administrators can direct traffic, configure networks, and enforce policies from a centralized SDN controller. This setup not only simplifies management but also provides comprehensive visibility across the network, facilitating more refined traffic handling.

Essential Components of SDN:

- **SDN Controller**: Serves as the network's brain, managing flow control to the routers and switches via a centralized platform.

- **Northbound APIs**: These interfaces allow applications on top of the SDN controller to communicate with it, enabling more dynamic network management.

- **Southbound APIs**: Protocols like OpenFlow define the communication between the controller and the network hardware, facilitating direct manipulation of the flow of data and the behavior of switches and routers.

Advantages of SDN:

- **Agility and Flexibility**: SDN provides the ability to swiftly adjust network practices to align with changing business environments, application needs, and user demands.

- **Scalability**: Centralized control simplifies expansion and adaptation of network infrastructures to support growth and new requirements.

- **Cost Reduction**: Decoupling control functions from specific hardware pieces allows for the use of less expensive commodity hardware and reduces dependency on proprietary systems.

- **Enhanced Security**: Centralized control also aids in the uniform application of security policies and quicker response to emerging threats.

Practical Applications:

- **Data Centers**: Managing data traffic efficiently, especially in environments like cloud services, where dynamic scaling and resource allocation are crucial.

- **Business Networks**: Streamlining operations and network management within corporate environments to support various business operations efficiently.

- **Network Function Virtualization (NFV)**: Complementing SDN, NFV replaces traditional network hardware functions with virtualized services running on the SDN infrastructure, like virtual firewalls and load balancers.

Challenges and Future Considerations:

- **Complex Integration**: Transitioning to SDN can be complex, requiring significant changes in the existing network architecture and operational practices.

- **Compatibility and Interoperability**: Ensuring that SDN technologies work seamlessly with existing network components and systems from various vendors is critical.

- **Security**: Centralization increases efficiency but also poses risks if the control plane is compromised, thus requiring robust protection mechanisms.

In summary, SDN is transforming network architecture with its flexible, efficient, and forward-looking approach, promising significant improvements in how networks are designed, operated, and managed.

10.5 The Importance of Network Function Virtualization (NFV)

Network Function Virtualization (NFV) is revolutionizing network management by separating network functions from proprietary hardware, allowing these functions to operate on generic servers across various network locations. This shift significantly influences network design and operations:

Foundational Concepts of NFV:

- **Definition**: NFV relocates network functions from specialized hardware to virtualized environments, running on standard servers. This transition from physical appliances, such as firewalls and load balancers, to software-based implementations offers a more flexible and dynamic networking approach.

- **Development**: The concept emerged from service providers aiming to reduce costs and enhance service flexibility, enabling quicker deployment of network services and maintenance.

Advantages of NFV:

- **Cost Reduction**: Transitioning to generic hardware reduces both upfront capital costs and ongoing operational expenses.

- **Enhanced Flexibility and Speed**: Network services can be deployed faster and adjusted more easily without the physical limitations of traditional hardware setups.

- **Scalability**: NFV improves the network's ability to scale operations smoothly as demand fluctuates.

Core Components of NFV:

- **NFV Infrastructure (NFVI)**: The combination of hardware and virtualization technologies that host the network functions.

- **Management and Orchestration (MANO)**: Frameworks that handle the setup, maintenance, and coordination of virtual network functions.

- **Virtual Network Functions (VNFs)**: These are the various network services, now running as software instances on the NFVI.

Challenges with NFV:

- **Management Complexity**: Orchestrating numerous virtual functions requires sophisticated management strategies.

- **Interoperability**: Integrating solutions from multiple vendors can present compatibility challenges.

- **Security**: Virtual environments necessitate new security strategies as traditional, centralized hardware-based defenses are no longer feasible.

Real-World Applications:

- **Telecommunications**: Telecom companies leverage NFV to efficiently roll out new services and adapt to changing network demands.

- **Enterprise Applications**: Companies use NFV to streamline network operations across distributed office locations, enhancing agility and reducing overhead.

Looking Ahead:

- **Integration with Advanced Technologies**: NFV is expected to synergize with Software-Defined Networking (SDN) and 5G networks, driving advancements like network slicing, which allows for multiple virtual networks to operate over a single physical network infrastructure.

NFV is paving the way for a more flexible, cost-efficient, and scalable network infrastructure, positioning itself as a cornerstone of modern network strategy, particularly as networks evolve towards more software-driven operations.

Chapter 11: Troubleshooting and Technical Support

11.1 Fundamental Troubleshooting Techniques

Here are the essential techniques used in network troubleshooting:

Understanding the Problem:

- **Clear Description**: Begin by clearly defining the issue. Note when the problem started and any changes in the network environment that coincided with the onset.

- **Symptom Identification**: Gather detailed information on symptoms and any error messages, which can help pinpoint the underlying issue.

Developing a Hypothesis:

- **Investigate Common Causes**: Examine usual suspects such as recent network changes, hardware malfunctions, or software updates.

- **Formulate Hypotheses**: Based on initial findings, hypothesize potential causes of the issue.

Testing the Hypothesis:

- **Replication**: Attempt to recreate the issue to observe the problem consistently, which aids in understanding the conditions causing it.

- **Systematic Examination**: Employ diagnostic tools and manual checks to validate your hypothesis and narrow down the cause.

Resolving the Issue:

- **Action Plan**: Develop a step-by-step plan to address the identified cause, considering the impact of potential solutions on network operations and users.

- **Implement Solutions**: Start with the least disruptive fixes that are likely to rectify the problem, always prepared with alternative solutions if the initial one fails.

Confirming and Preventing Future Issues:

- **Verification**: Once a solution is implemented, confirm with users that the issue is resolved and that the network is fully functional.

- **Preventative Measures**: Reflect on the root cause and implement measures to prevent recurrence, which might include updates to network configuration, documentation enhancements, or improved monitoring.

Documentation and Knowledge Sharing:

- **Record Keeping**: Document the issue's details, troubleshooting steps taken, and the final outcome. This record is invaluable for future troubleshooting and training.

- **Sharing Insights**: Disseminate lessons learned and effective solutions among the team or through organizational knowledge bases to facilitate quicker resolution of similar issues in the future.

These structured steps ensure thorough handling of network issues, from initial problem identification to resolution and prevention, streamlining the troubleshooting process and enhancing network reliability.

11.2 Solving Common Network Problems

Network administrators often face a variety of common network issues that can disrupt connectivity and degrade performance. Effective troubleshooting and resolution strategies are essential to maintain optimal network functionality. Here's a streamlined approach to tackling typical network challenges:

Connectivity Issues:

- **Symptoms**: Devices failing to connect, experiencing intermittent connections, or suffering from slow network speeds.

- **Solutions**:

    - Inspect physical connections like cables and ports for damage or disconnection.

    - Verify network settings including IP addresses and DNS configurations are correct.

    - Reboot routers and switches to resolve temporary glitches.

    - Update network drivers and firmware to address compatibility issues and bugs.

IP Address Conflicts:

- **Symptoms**: Network disturbances due to multiple devices assigned the same IP address.

- **Solutions**:

    - Configure devices to receive IP addresses automatically via DHCP to avoid manual configuration errors.

    - Review DHCP server settings to ensure it's not allocating already in-use addresses.

    - Release and renew IP addresses on the conflicting devices.

Slow Internet Speeds:

- **Symptoms**: Lagging performance accessing online resources, slow download or upload speeds.

- **Solutions**:

    - Monitor and manage the use of bandwidth-heavy applications.

    - Perform speed tests to confirm if the Internet service provider (ISP) is delivering promised speeds.

- Adjust router settings, such as altering channels or bands, to minimize interference and enhance performance.

Network Overloads:

- **Symptoms:** Network failures or significant slowdowns due to excessive usage.

- **Solutions:**

  - Apply Quality of Service (QoS) rules to prioritize essential traffic and control bandwidth for less critical applications.

  - Consider upgrading network infrastructure to support greater data demands.

  - Utilize network monitoring tools to pinpoint and manage high traffic sources.

Wireless Issues - Interference and Range:

- **Symptoms:** Inconsistent wireless signal strength, frequent disconnections, or dead zones.

- **Solutions:**

  - Switch to a less congested wireless channel.

  - Position routers and access points strategically, avoiding obstructions and interference sources like microwaves.

  - Expand coverage using additional access points or range extenders.

Security Breaches:

- **Symptoms:** Unauthorized access, data breaches, or malware infections.

- **Solutions:**

  - Keep network systems updated and patched to secure vulnerabilities.

  - Educate network users on security best practices and implement robust authentication methods.

Hardware Failures:

- **Symptoms:** Unexpected network outages, device malfunctions, or visible damage.

- **Solutions:**

  - Conduct regular hardware inspections and maintenance.

  - Prepare for hardware failures with backup systems or devices to ensure quick replacements.

  - Diagnose and remedy hardware issues promptly using appropriate tools.

This structured approach not only helps in resolving current issues but also in preventing future disruptions, ensuring the network remains robust and efficient.

11.3 Advanced Tools for Network Troubleshooting

Network troubleshooting can be greatly enhanced by using advanced tools designed to diagnose and resolve complex issues. These tools enable deeper insights into network operations and assist in pinpointing problems effectively. Here's an overview of several key tools and their applications in network management:

1. Packet Analyzers:

- **Example**: Wireshark

- **Functionality**: These tools capture and analyze packets flowing through the network, helping to inspect traffic details, troubleshoot protocol issues, and monitor network health at a detailed level.

- **Usage**: Particularly useful for debugging network functions, ensuring security compliance, and monitoring data flows for abnormal activities.

2. Network Scanners:

- **Example**: Nmap

- **Functionality**: Network scanners are instrumental in mapping network infrastructure, identifying active devices and open ports, and evaluating network security.

- **Usage**: Ideal for security assessments, network inventory management, and identifying potential vulnerabilities.

3. Network Performance Monitors (NPMs):

- **Example**: SolarWinds Network Performance Monitor

- **Functionality**: NPMs track critical performance metrics like bandwidth utilization, latency, and packet loss. They provide visual feedback and alerts to identify and troubleshoot network performance issues.

- **Usage**: Crucial for maintaining optimal network performance, identifying bottlenecks, and proactive network management.

4. Application Performance Management (APM) Tools:

- **Example**: Dynatrace

- **Functionality**: APM tools offer monitoring and management of application performance, ensuring that applications are running smoothly and efficiently across the network.

- **Usage**: Essential in environments where network performance directly impacts application functionality and user experience.

5. Automation Platforms:

- **Example**: Ansible

- **Functionality**: These platforms automate routine network management tasks, reducing manual intervention and minimizing human errors.

- **Usage**: Useful for automating deployment, configurations, and routine network maintenance tasks across various network devices.

6. Wireless Network Troubleshooting Tools:

- **Example**: AirMagnet WiFi Analyzer

- **Functionality**: Specialized in analyzing and optimizing the performance of wireless networks, these tools assess signal strength, detect interference, and secure wireless communications.

- **Usage**: Indispensable for ensuring robust wireless connectivity, especially in complex environments with multiple overlapping wireless signals.

7. Root Cause Analysis Software:

- **Example**: Splunk

- **Functionality**: These tools aggregate and analyze data from various network and application sources to trace the root causes of network disruptions or failures.

- **Usage**: Particularly valuable in complex network environments where pinpointing the exact cause of a problem requires correlating large volumes of data from various sources.

Together, these tools form a comprehensive suite for network administrators to monitor, manage, and resolve issues within their networks, ensuring high uptime and optimal performance.

11.4 The Role of Technical Support

Technical support is indispensable for the smooth operation of network systems, providing vital assistance to users and ensuring networks perform optimally. Here's an exploration of the fundamental roles and contributions of technical support teams in network management:

1. Problem Solving:

- **Immediate Assistance**: Technical support acts as the initial point of contact for users facing issues, offering quick fixes or escalating complex problems to specialist teams.

- **Detailed Troubleshooting**: They apply structured troubleshooting methods to diagnose and resolve issues, minimizing downtime and ensuring continuous productivity.

2. Support and Education:

- **User Assistance**: Support staff assist users with routine questions and minor issues related to network services and software operations.

- **Instructional Content**: They create and distribute tutorials and documentation that help users navigate and utilize network resources more effectively.

3. System Maintenance:

- **Regular Monitoring**: Ongoing duties include overseeing network performance to preemptively address potential failures.

- **Updates and Patches**: Ensuring that network systems and applications are up-to-date with the latest software patches is crucial for maintaining security and functionality.

4. Documentation and Analytics:

- **Record-Keeping**: Maintaining precise records of technical issues and user interactions helps in tracking trends and refining future troubleshooting efforts.

- **Reporting**: They compile reports detailing network performance and support activities, which are essential for operational oversight and strategic planning.

5. Security Oversight:

- **Security Implementations**: Technical support teams play a crucial role in setting up and managing network security measures to safeguard sensitive data.

- **Proactive Monitoring**: They also monitor network systems for security threats and coordinate responses to security incidents to protect network integrity.

6. User Feedback Integration:

- **Improvement Initiatives**: Gathering and analyzing user feedback is key to enhancing network services and support strategies.

- **Team Collaboration**: Technical support frequently collaborates with network engineers to suggest system improvements and resolve recurrent issues based on user feedback and observed trends.

7. Emergency Management:

- **Crisis Handling**: In critical situations, such as major network outages or security breaches, technical support coordinates rapid response efforts to mitigate damage and communicate effectively with affected parties.

Technical support teams are essential for not just resolving immediate technical issues but also for contributing to the long-term health and evolution of network infrastructures. Their ability to quickly address problems, coupled with their ongoing maintenance and security efforts, plays a pivotal role in maintaining network reliability and user satisfaction.

11.5 Preventative Measures and Routine Maintenance

Preventative measures and routine maintenance are strategies for maintaining network efficiency and minimizing the risk of unexpected system failures or security breaches. These practices are essential for sustaining network reliability and optimal performance:

1. **Regular Updates and Patch Management:**

   - **System Updates:** It's crucial to keep all network devices and software up-to-date, including the latest firmware for routers and switches, and software patches for operating systems and applications.

   - **Vulnerability Management:** Promptly applying security patches to address known vulnerabilities is critical. Utilizing patch management tools can help automate this process and ensure consistent updates across all systems.

2. **Hardware Inspections and Upgrades:**

   - **Routine Inspections:** Regular checks of physical hardware for signs of wear or damage are essential for early identification of potential issues.

   - **Hardware Upgrades:** Regularly planning for hardware upgrades prevents the challenges associated with aging infrastructure, such as increased failure rates and compatibility issues.

3. **Network Performance Monitoring:**

   - **Continuous Monitoring:** Monitoring tools are used to continuously observe performance metrics to spot potential issues like latency increases, bandwidth bottlenecks, or unusual traffic patterns.

   - **Proactive Alerts:** Configuring alerts to notify IT staff about potential issues helps in addressing problems before they impact network performance or user experience.

4. **Backup and Disaster Recovery:**

   - **Regular Backups:** Implementing a strong backup strategy is crucial, involving regular backups of critical data and system configurations, stored securely both on-site and off-site.

   - **Disaster Recovery Plans:** Having a well-defined disaster recovery plan ensures quick restoration of operations following disruptions, from hardware failures to natural disasters.

5. **Security Measures:**

   - **Firewalls and Intrusion Detection:** Keeping firewalls and intrusion detection/prevention systems up to date is necessary to guard against malicious activities.

   - **Security Audits:** Periodic security audits are important for assessing the effectiveness of existing security measures and identifying necessary improvements.

6. **Documentation and Configuration Management:**

   - **Accurate Documentation:** Maintaining detailed records of network configurations and hardware inventories is crucial for effective troubleshooting and recovery after incidents.

- **Configuration Baselines:** Establishing and maintaining configuration baselines aids in ensuring consistent settings across network devices and simplifies recovery processes.

7. **Staff Training and Awareness:**

   - **Ongoing Training:** Regular training for IT staff on the latest network management practices and emerging threats ensures that the team is knowledgeable and prepared.

   - **User Awareness:** Conducting regular sessions on cybersecurity best practices for all network users enhances the overall security posture by raising awareness about the importance of updates and security protocols.

11.6 Effective Documentation and Knowledge Sharing

Effective documentation and knowledge ensure that critical information is readily available, promoting a more informed and cohesive IT environment. Here's how organizations can successfully foster these practices:

1. **Comprehensive Documentation Practices:**

   - **Network Diagrams:** Keep updated visual representations of the network's layout to help in understanding and managing its setup.

   - **Configuration Documentation:** Maintain records of settings for all network devices, ensuring configurations are well-documented and easy to replicate or revert if needed.

   - **Change Management Logs:** Log every change within the network, including details about what was changed, who changed it, and the reason for the change. This historical data is invaluable for tracking and understanding the impacts of modifications.

2. **Standard Operating Procedures (SOPs):**

   - **Guidelines:** Establish and document SOPs for routine and corrective maintenance, ensuring consistent execution of tasks and simplifying training processes.

   - **Regular Updates:** Continually refine SOPs to incorporate new technologies, insights from previous incidents, and adjustments in network strategies or policies.

3. **Knowledge Base Development:**

   - **Solution Repository:** Develop a centralized location where solutions to frequent problems, best practices, and guidance are stored. This should be a dynamic tool that grows with new insights and solutions.

   - **Encourage Contributions:** Foster a culture where all team members actively contribute to the knowledge base, enriching it with their unique experiences and solutions.

4. **Training and Workshops:**

   - **Continuous Learning:** Regular training sessions should be held to update the team on network procedures, recent changes, and effective troubleshooting techniques.

- **Collaborative Workshops**: Organize interactive sessions where team members can share experiences, discuss challenges, and collectively explore solutions, thereby enhancing team cohesion and skill.

5. **Utilizing Collaboration Tools**:

   - **Platforms for Team Interaction**: Implement collaborative tools that support seamless communication and the sharing of information, such as Microsoft Teams, Slack, or Confluence.

   - **Accessibility of Documentation**: Ensure all documentation is easily accessible to everyone in the team, preferably stored in cloud-based systems for easy retrieval and editing.

6. **Feedback Mechanisms**:

   - **Iterative Improvement**: Set up processes to regularly gather feedback on the documentation and knowledge-sharing practices to continually refine and improve these resources.

7. **Incentivizing Knowledge Sharing**:

   - **Recognition Programs**: Establish recognition and rewards systems to encourage and celebrate contributions to the collective knowledge base and documentation efforts.

By integrating these strategies, organizations can ensure that their network management teams are equipped with the knowledge and tools necessary to maintain a robust and efficient network infrastructure.

Chapter 12: Networking Across Industries

12.1 Networking Solutions for Small and Medium Enterprises

Networking solutions for small and medium enterprises (SMEs) are tailored to meet the unique challenges these businesses face, such as operating with limited budgets and IT resources, while still needing robust systems to support their operations. Here are several approaches SMEs can take to ensure their networking is effective, affordable, and scalable:

- **Cloud-Based Services**: SMEs can take advantage of cloud services to reduce the need for expensive onsite equipment. Options like cloud storage and software-as-a-service offer scalable resources that adapt to changing needs without a hefty upfront investment.

- **Virtual Private Networks (VPNs)**: VPNs offer a cost-effective way to secure remote connections, allowing employees safe access to business data from anywhere. This is especially valuable for companies with remote or mobile workforces.

- **Managed Service Providers (MSPs)**: SMEs can benefit from outsourcing their network management to MSPs. This allows businesses to focus on core activities without needing a large in-house IT team, as MSPs handle maintenance, updates, and security.

- **Integrated Solutions**: Opting for integrated solutions that combine both wireless and wired networking with built-in security features can simplify the network setup and reduce the need for multiple devices.

- **Scalability**: Implementing modular solutions that can be easily adjusted or expanded ensures that businesses only pay for what they need when they need it. Hybrid models that combine on-premises and cloud infrastructure can also provide flexibility and facilitate growth.

- **Robust Security Measures**: Despite budget constraints, it's crucial for SMEs to enforce strong security measures to protect sensitive data. This includes setting up firewalls, using anti-malware tools, and complying with relevant data protection regulations.

- **Network Performance Monitoring**: Utilizing tools that monitor network performance helps businesses preemptively address issues, maintain system health, and optimize operations. Many affordable monitoring tools provide valuable insights into network usage and system performance.

- **Professional Consulting**: While not a daily requirement, occasional investment in professional consulting services for network setup or major upgrades can help SMEs avoid costly mistakes and ensure that their network aligns with both current and future business needs.

For SMEs, building a network that is affordable, secure, and capable of adapting to growth is key. This not only supports current operations but also paves the way for seamless expansion as business needs evolve.

12.2 Corporate Networking Case Studies

In the corporate landscape, the deployment of sophisticated networking solutions is vital for supporting complex operations and strategic goals. Below are several case studies that demonstrate how companies from various sectors have effectively utilized advanced networking technologies to enhance operational efficiency, bolster security, and manage costs:

- **Global Retail Corporation**: This corporation faced challenges with securing data and ensuring reliable network connections across its worldwide outlets, including in regions with poor connectivity. By adopting a hybrid network model that combines MPLS (Multi-Protocol Label Switching) and SD-WAN (Software-Defined Wide Area Network), the company enhanced its bandwidth and reliability. The SD-WAN technology provided smart path selection and bandwidth optimization, leading to improved network uptime, cost reduction by using more affordable connectivity options, and better security across global operations.

- **Financial Services Firm**: To address network security and compliance challenges, a financial firm implemented an advanced network segmentation strategy. Using VLANs (Virtual Local Area Networks) and strict network access control (NAC) systems, along with robust intrusion detection systems (IDS) and compliance audits, the firm managed to streamline regulatory compliance and strengthen its network against security threats. This meticulous setup safeguarded sensitive financial data and upheld the integrity and confidentiality of client information.

- **Healthcare Provider Network**: A major healthcare provider needed to ensure the high availability and secure access to medical records across its network, which includes several hospitals and clinics. By deploying an NFV (Network Function Virtualization)-based infrastructure, the provider could flexibly scale network functions as services according to demand. Strong encryption and multi-factor authentication were employed to secure patient data, enhancing care quality and meeting health data regulations.

- **Technology Start-Up**: A fast-growing tech start-up required a scalable and economical networking solution to support its burgeoning operations without substantial upfront capital expenditure. Opting for a cloud-based networking model, the start-up leveraged public cloud services for both computing and network needs. This approach allowed for automatic resource adjustments based on demand, fostering rapid growth and innovation by facilitating the easy testing of new configurations and services.

These case studies highlight the importance of choosing the right networking strategies and technologies to address specific business needs and challenges, demonstrating that with thoughtful implementation, businesses can achieve significant improvements in performance, security, and scalability.

12.3 Networking for Smart Cities

Smart cities utilize cutting-edge information and communication technologies and a vast network of interconnected devices to enhance urban functionality and improve residents' quality of life. Here's a look at how networking drives this innovation:

- **IoT Integration**: Smart cities employ extensive IoT networks that connect everything from traffic sensors to streetlights, facilitating efficient urban management. For example, traffic sensors can monitor flow and adjust signals in real-time, helping to ease congestion and reduce emissions.

- **Advanced Communication Systems**: The backbone of smart city operations, high-speed internet connections like broadband and fiber optics, support the immense data demands of urban applications. Additionally, the deployment of 5G networks is critical for enabling technologies that require high data throughput and minimal latency, such as autonomous vehicles and real-time urban management systems.

- **Cloud and Edge Computing**: Smart cities often rely on cloud services for scalable computing and storage solutions, accommodating the extensive data processing involved. Edge computing complements this by processing data locally, reducing latency, and speeding up response times for critical applications.

- **Enhanced Security and Privacy**: With the network's pivotal role in smart cities, robust security measures are essential to protect data integrity and citizen privacy. This involves implementing advanced cybersecurity measures and developing policies to ensure data privacy and ethical usage.

- **Sustainability and Resilience**: Networking infrastructure in smart cities is designed not only for efficiency but also sustainability. Smart energy systems, such as intelligent grids, optimize energy use across the city. Moreover, these networks are crucial in disaster management, providing essential data that enhances emergency responses and recovery efforts.

- **Public Connectivity**: Expansive public Wi-Fi networks enhance connectivity, enabling residents and visitors to access various city services through mobile applications seamlessly and remain connected in public spaces.

- **Interoperability Standards**: To ensure seamless operation among diverse technologies and platforms within a smart city, standardization is vital. This standardization ensures different systems and devices can communicate effectively, supporting a cohesive and functional urban environment.

Smart cities represent a convergence of technology and urban management, promising more efficient, sustainable, and livable urban environments through innovative networking solutions.

12.4 Networking in Educational Settings

Networking in educational environments is essential for fostering a dynamic learning atmosphere and streamlining both academic and administrative activities. As digital technologies become more entrenched in educational systems, a strong network infrastructure is vital to support e-learning platforms, virtual classrooms, and a broad array of online resources. Here's a deeper look into the critical networking components within educational settings:

Campus-Wide Wi-Fi Connectivity

- **Accessibility:** It's crucial for educational institutions to offer extensive Wi-Fi coverage across campuses, ensuring students and faculty have access to digital resources in various locations, including classrooms, libraries, dormitories, and outdoor areas.

- **Challenges:** Managing such expansive Wi-Fi networks involves addressing issues related to high user density, bandwidth allocation, and maintaining reliable connectivity throughout diverse and complex campus structures.

E-Learning Platforms and Online Resources

- **Digital Learning Support:** Institutions rely heavily on e-learning systems like Moodle and Blackboard, which require stable, high-speed internet to operate efficiently.

- **Bandwidth for Content Streaming:** The demand for streaming educational content such as video lectures increases the need for networks with substantial data handling capabilities.

Network Security

- **Protecting Sensitive Data:** Networks in educational settings must safeguard sensitive information like student records and financial data, adhering to regulations such as FERPA.

- **Access Controls:** Implementing effective user authentication systems ensures that only authorized users can access certain network resources, enhancing security and privacy.

Administrative Efficiency

- **Resource Management:** Networks enable more efficient management of essential resources, facilitating tasks such as online registration, scheduling, and facility access control.

- **Communication Tools:** Robust networks support various communication platforms essential for daily interactions among students and staff, including emails, messaging apps, and VoIP services.

Scalability and Flexibility

- **Adapting to Growth:** As educational institutions evolve, so must their networks. Scalable solutions are necessary to support an increasing number of users and devices without compromising network performance.

- **Supporting New Technologies:** Networks must also be flexible to accommodate emerging technologies and shifts in educational practices, including the adoption of IoT devices in classrooms.

Ensuring Digital Equity

- **Access for All:** Schools are pivotal in bridging the digital divide, ensuring that all students have equitable access to technology and the internet, which may include providing network resources to students lacking reliable internet access at home.

Preparedness for Emergencies

- **Crisis Management:** In emergencies, such as natural disasters or security incidents, reliable networking is crucial for effective communication and managing security systems.

Sustainability Practices

- **Energy Efficiency:** Educational institutions increasingly strive to optimize their network infrastructures for energy efficiency, reducing their overall environmental impact and supporting sustainability goals.

12.5 Challenges of Networking in Healthcare

Networking within healthcare settings involves navigating unique complexities due to the essential nature of medical services, the need for high data security, and the integration of diverse technology. Here are the main challenges healthcare networks face:

Data Security and Privacy

- **Strict Regulations:** Healthcare networks must adhere to stringent regulations like HIPAA, which demand rigorous data protection measures.

- **Cybersecurity Risks:** Given the value of medical information, healthcare networks are frequent targets for cyber-attacks, necessitating robust security protocols and vigilant monitoring.

High Availability and Reliability

- **Vital Medical Services:** Network failures can jeopardize critical services like patient record access and telemedicine, making reliability and uptime paramount.

- **Redundancy Requirements:** Networks in healthcare must have fail-safe systems and backups to maintain functionality continuously.

Integration of Diverse Medical Devices

- **Complex Device Ecosystem:** Healthcare networks support everything from wearable devices to advanced diagnostic equipment, requiring comprehensive interoperability and seamless connectivity.

- **Compatibility Challenges:** Ensuring diverse medical technologies work together without issues is an ongoing challenge.

Scalability

- **Keeping Pace with Innovation:** Healthcare technology evolves rapidly, necessitating networks that can expand swiftly to support new applications and increased data flows.

- **Adaptable Architecture:** Network infrastructure must be versatile to accommodate growing demands and technological advancements without extensive overhauls.

Mobile and Remote Access

- **Expansion of Telemedicine:** Networks must support secure and reliable remote healthcare services, which have become especially crucial.

- **Remote Data Access:** Ensuring that healthcare professionals can securely access patient data offsite poses significant security challenges.

Regulatory Compliance

- **Regulatory Evolution:** Healthcare providers must stay abreast of new and changing regulations concerning data protection and patient privacy.

- **Compliance Costs:** Meeting these regulatory requirements often involves substantial investment, both for initial implementation and for ongoing compliance verification.

Budget Constraints

- **Financial Limitations:** Many healthcare providers face strict budgeting constraints, complicating the funding of necessary network upgrades or expansions.

- **Balancing Costs:** Decision-makers often need to weigh the costs against the potential benefits of network investments, seeking the most cost-effective solutions without compromising essential services.

Training and Awareness

- **Continuous Education:** Training healthcare and IT staff to use network resources responsibly and securely is crucial for minimizing risks and ensuring smooth operations.

- **Awareness Programs:** Regular updates and education on security best practices can help mitigate the risk of data breaches and ensure compliance with healthcare regulations.

12.6 Government Infrastructure Networking

Networking within government infrastructure is pivotal due to the critical nature of public services, necessitating high security, and robust communications. Here are several aspects of how governments manage and implement their networks:

High Security and Data Protection

- **Robust Cybersecurity Measures:** Governments must employ advanced security protocols like encryption, firewalls, and intrusion detection systems to safeguard sensitive data against threats.

- **Regulatory Adherence:** Compliance with strict regulatory standards is essential for the protection, handling, and sharing of data, necessitating regular security audits and updates.

Scalable and Resilient Infrastructure

- **Redundancy and Failover Systems:** Essential for maintaining uninterrupted services, government networks require robust redundancy plans and backup communication paths.

- **Scalability:** Government networks must adapt and scale efficiently as digital services expand and new technologies are integrated.

Interdepartmental Connectivity and Collaboration

- **Unified Network Solutions:** To enhance cooperation among various government sectors, networks must support seamless data sharing and interconnectivity.

- **Secure Remote Access:** Especially critical during emergencies or for routine remote work, networks must provide secure and reliable connections for government personnel.

Public Access Networks

- **Public Wi-Fi Accessibility:** Providing secure and high-capacity public Wi-Fi in places like parks and public buildings is increasingly common, supporting community access to digital services.

- **Digital Inclusion Initiatives:** Expanding network access to underserved communities is crucial for ensuring equitable access to government services and resources.

Emergency and Disaster Communication

- **Robust Disaster Response Networks:** Networks must remain operational in extreme conditions to ensure effective communication during emergencies.

- **Mobile and Deployable Solutions:** Temporary and mobile network solutions are vital during crises where standard infrastructure is disrupted.

Smart City Technologies

- **Integration of IoT Devices:** Implementing IoT in smart city initiatives helps enhance urban management through traffic systems, environmental monitoring, and more.

- **Advanced Data Analytics:** Networks must handle extensive data from smart technologies, requiring significant processing power to analyze and utilize this information effectively.

Challenges and Constraints

- **Budget Limitations:** Financial constraints often impact the ability to upgrade or expand network infrastructure comprehensively.

- **Balancing Security and Transparency:** Ensuring network security while maintaining the public's right to information access and transparency is an ongoing challenge.

This framework highlights the necessity for dynamic, secure, and resilient networking to support the essential functions and services provided by government bodies, ensuring that public needs and safety are effectively met.

Chapter 13: Advancing Your Networking Career

13.1 Understanding the Networking Profession

The networking profession involves designing, implementing, managing, and maintaining the infrastructure that allows devices to connect to the Internet and communicate with each other. This field is foundational to virtually every aspect of modern business and technology, making it both dynamic and essential. Understanding the networking profession involves recognizing its scope, the roles it encompasses, and the impact it has on the world.

1. Scope of the Profession:

- **Core Responsibilities:** Professionals in networking ensure that data flows smoothly across digital and telecommunication networks. This includes tasks like network design, installation, administration, and troubleshooting to keep systems operational and secure.

- **Vital Industries:** Networking professionals work across various industries including IT services, telecommunications, healthcare, finance, and government. Their work supports critical services such as internet access, cloud computing, data center operations, and cybersecurity.

2. Roles and Specializations:

- **Network Technician:** Entry-level position focusing on the maintenance and repair of networking equipment.

- **Network Engineer:** Designs and implements network configurations, troubleshoots performance issues, and ensures network security.

- **Network Administrator:** Manages daily operations of networks, ensuring reliability and stability.

- **Network Architect:** Develops broad network infrastructures that support organizational goals and integrates new technologies.

- **Cybersecurity Specialist:** Focuses on protecting networks from threats and implementing security protocols.

3. Impact on Technology and Business:

- **Enabling Connectivity:** Networking professionals enable connectivity, a fundamental requirement for all modern digital interactions, supporting everything from e-commerce and global communications to cloud applications and the Internet of Things (IoT).

- **Supporting Innovation:** As advocates and implementers of the latest technology trends, networking professionals help to drive innovations in fields like 5G, smart cities, and more, paving the way for new products and services.

4. Challenges and Rewards:

- **Constant Learning:** The field requires ongoing learning and adaptation to keep pace with rapidly changing technologies. Professionals must continuously update their skills through certifications and training.

- **Problem Solving:** The role often involves critical problem-solving under pressure, particularly when dealing with network outages or security breaches that can have significant repercussions.

- **Career Growth and Opportunities:** Due to the essential nature of networking, there are significant opportunities for career advancement and specialization. The profession offers a clear pathway from technical roles to managerial positions.

5. Essential Skills:

- **Technical Skills:** Proficiency in network technologies such as TCP/IP, routing protocols, network simulation, and configuration management.

- **Soft Skills:** Strong problem-solving abilities, attention to detail, and communication skills are crucial for effectively explaining technology solutions to non-technical stakeholders.

13.2 Educational Pathways in Networking

A successful career in networking generally starts with a solid educational background in fields like computer science or information technology. Here's an outline of the educational routes that can prepare individuals for a thriving career in this sector:

Foundational Education

- **Degrees:** Associate's and bachelor's degrees in computer science or IT lay the groundwork, offering a broad curriculum that includes network security, system design, and programming. For those aiming at specialized roles, such as network architect, or leadership positions, pursuing advanced degrees like a master's in network engineering is beneficial.

Certification Programs

- **Cisco Certifications:** Earning a Cisco Certified Network Associate (CCNA) or Cisco Certified Network Professional (CCNP) is highly esteemed within the industry. These certifications demonstrate one's capability in handling essential network tasks.

- **CompTIA Network+:** This entry-level certification is ideal for beginners and covers basic networking concepts, infrastructure, and operations.

- **CISSP:** The Certified Information Systems Security Professional certification is geared towards professionals focusing on network security, underscoring their expertise in securing a network environment.

Alternative Learning Paths

- **Online Learning:** Platforms like Coursera and Udemy offer a range of courses on network fundamentals and advanced topics such as cybersecurity and cloud networking, which are accessible and can be tailored to individual pace and interest.

- **Bootcamps:** These intensive training programs provide hands-on experience and are particularly useful for rapid skill acquisition in specialized areas like network security.

Continued Education and Networking

- **Professional Development:** Regular workshops and seminars are crucial for keeping up with rapid technological advancements and industry shifts.

- **Networking and Community Engagement:** Joining professional organizations such as IEEE or the Internet Society can offer networking opportunities, access to professional development tools, and a deeper insight into the industry.

Independent Learning

- **Self-directed Study:** Keeping abreast of the latest industry trends, technologies, and best practices through journals, blogs, and forums is essential for continual professional growth and relevance.

13.3 Gaining Practical Experience

Gaining practical experience in the networking field is crucial, helping bridge the gap between academic studies and real-world applications. Here are effective ways to acquire hands-on experience in networking:

Internships

- **Real-World Application:** Internships provide practical exposure by placing you in settings where you can apply academic knowledge under guidance, often leading to job opportunities.

- **Professional Networking:** They also offer a chance to connect with professionals and learn from their experiences, expanding your industry insight.

Apprenticeships

- **In-depth Training:** Apprenticeships involve comprehensive, on-the-job training under expert supervision, integrating employment and education in technology fields like networking.

- **Certification Opportunities:** These programs often support earning professional certifications, boosting both skills and employability.

Freelancing and Part-Time Jobs

- **Varied Experience:** Engaging in freelance projects or part-time work allows handling diverse networking challenges, enhancing adaptability and problem-solving skills.

- **Portfolio Development:** Successfully completed projects build up a portfolio, demonstrating your capabilities to prospective employers.

Simulations and Virtual Labs

- **Skill Practice**: Tools such as Cisco Packet Tracer or GNS3 enable simulation of networking environments where you can practice without the need for expensive hardware.

- **Understanding Complex Systems**: These platforms are valuable for testing network setups and troubleshooting in a controlled, consequence-free environment.

Volunteering

- **Community Contribution**: Offering your networking skills to non-profits or educational institutions not only supports these organizations but also enriches your experience.

- **Professional Growth**: Volunteering can also enhance your resume and provide you with commendable references.

Participation in Projects and Collaborative Work

- **Professional Engagement**: Joining projects, especially in your current role or through professional networks, exposes you to new technologies and larger deployments.

- **Team Skills**: Collaborating across various IT disciplines helps understand the broader context of networking within IT infrastructures.

Hackathons and Competitions

- **Learning Under Pressure**: Competitions that focus on networking challenge you to solve practical problems quickly, a great way to sharpen your skills.

- **Recognition**: Achievements in these contests can be notable additions to your resume, highlighting your skills and commitment to your profession.

Each of these pathways offers unique benefits and learning opportunities, crucial for developing a comprehensive skill set in networking.

13.4 Strategies for Career Advancement

Advancing in the networking profession involves more than just technical expertise; it requires a commitment to continuous improvement, strategic career planning, and broadening your skill set. Here's how you can move forward in your networking career:

Continuous Education and Certification

- Stay Updated: The field of networking is continually evolving with new technologies. Engaging in ongoing education through specialized courses, webinars, and industry certifications keeps you competitive and knowledgeable.

- Obtain Advanced Certifications: Certifications in specialized areas like cloud networking, cybersecurity, or advanced network engineering (e.g., CCIE) can open doors to higher-level positions and distinguish you from your peers.

Professional Networking and Mentorship

- Engage with the Community: Active participation in industry conferences, workshops, and seminars helps build a robust professional network. Joining organizations like the IEEE Communications Society can further enhance your networking opportunities.

- Seek Mentorship: A mentor can offer invaluable guidance and insight, helping you navigate your career path more effectively.

Diversifying Experience

- Expand Your Skills: Gain experience in adjacent areas such as cybersecurity, cloud services, or systems administration. This versatility can make you indispensable within an organization.

- Leadership Roles: Take the initiative to lead projects. Leading teams or projects not only increases your visibility within the company but also hones your leadership skills.

Demonstrate Your Expertise

- Build a Portfolio: Documenting your achievements and project involvements in a professional portfolio can highlight your expertise and successes.

- Share Knowledge: Writing articles or speaking at industry events can establish you as a thought leader and add significant value to your professional profile.

Strategic Career Moves

- Plan Your Career Path: Strategically plan your career moves to ensure each step contributes to your long-term goals.

- Leverage Internal Opportunities: Explore opportunities for advancement within your current organization which could offer new challenges and learning opportunities.

Soft Skills Development

- Enhance Communication: Effective communication is crucial, particularly in roles that involve stakeholder engagement or team management.

- Problem-solving: Sharpen your problem-solving skills, as these are crucial for troubleshooting and innovating within your role.

Building Your Personal Brand

- Maintain an Online Presence: A professional online presence on platforms like LinkedIn reflects your career achievements and skills to potential employers or collaborators.

- Personal Branding: Ensure consistency across all professional platforms to maintain a strong personal brand that accurately reflects your career progression and expertise.

Leadership Preparation

- Develop Leadership Skills: As you aim for higher positions, focus on cultivating strong leadership qualities, including strategic decision-making and effective team management.

- Innovate: Showcasing your ability to drive innovation and improve processes can set you apart as a leader in the networking field.

By following these strategies, you can build a fulfilling career in networking that not only spans a wide range of technologies and industries but also positions you as a leader in the field.

13.5 Opportunities in Emerging Networking Fields

The networking profession is continuously evolving, with new technologies leading to the creation of specialized fields. These advancements offer exciting career opportunities for professionals looking to expand their expertise. Here are several emerging areas in networking that are gaining traction:

Software-Defined Networking (SDN) and Network Functions Virtualization (NFV): These technologies are revolutionizing how networks are managed and operated, making them more flexible and efficient. Professionals can explore roles such as SDN/NFV Network Architects, Integration Specialists, and Operations Managers.

Cybersecurity: This ever-important field is expanding as the need for enhanced security measures grows across all networking sectors. Opportunities range from Network Security Engineers to Chief Security Officers, all focused on safeguarding network data and systems against cyber threats.

Internet of Things (IoT): The exponential growth of connected devices has created a demand for specialists who can ensure these devices communicate securely and efficiently. Positions in this area include IoT Specialists, Security Analysts, and Network Engineers with a focus on IoT systems.

Cloud Networking: With the shift towards cloud-based operations, expertise in cloud networking is highly valued. Roles such as Cloud Network Engineers, Cloud Architects, and Cloud Services Developers are essential in designing and maintaining cloud infrastructure.

5G Technology: The deployment of 5G networks offers new possibilities for mobile and fixed wireless networking, requiring skilled professionals to develop and maintain these advanced networks. Roles include 5G Network Engineers and Infrastructure Specialists.

Artificial Intelligence and Machine Learning in Networking: AI and ML are being integrated to automate network management and enhance efficiency. Careers in this area include specialists in AI-driven analytics and Machine Learning Engineers who work on algorithms to improve network operations.

Edge Computing: As data processing moves closer to the data source, edge computing demands network professionals who can manage its distributed nature. Emerging roles include Edge Network Managers and Edge Solutions Architects.

These fields highlight the dynamic nature of the networking profession and underscore the opportunities for professionals to specialize in cutting-edge technologies that shape the future of networking.

13.6 Keeping Competitive in the Networking Industry

To stay competitive in the networking industry, professionals must be proactive about their career development, prioritize continual learning, and adapt to the latest technological changes. Here's a strategic approach to maintaining a competitive edge:

Continuous Learning and Certification: Stay relevant by maintaining up-to-date certifications and consider pursuing advanced degrees in specialized fields such as cybersecurity or network management. This not only enhances your skill set but also showcases your commitment to staying ahead in your field.

Embracing New Technologies: Keep abreast of emerging technologies like SDN, NFV, IoT, and 5G. Gain hands-on experience through personal projects or participation in beta testing, which can provide practical knowledge and an early adopter advantage.

Networking and Community Engagement: Active participation in professional networks and industry associations is crucial. Attend conferences and workshops to stay informed about the latest trends and to network with peers and industry leaders.

Developing Soft Skills: Enhance your leadership and communication skills. These are vital for career advancement, especially in roles involving team leadership or stakeholder management.

Research and Innovation: Stay informed about the latest research and contribute to innovation within the field. Engaging in writing, speaking, or creating projects can establish you as a thought leader.

Strategic Career Planning: Set clear career goals and regularly assess your skills against industry demands. Identify skills gaps and seek out training or projects to address these areas.

Adaptability: In an industry characterized by rapid change, the ability to adapt to new technologies and methodologies is essential. Cultivate flexibility and resilience to navigate shifts in technology and the workplace effectively.

By integrating these strategies, networking professionals can enhance their marketability and achieve sustained success in an ever-evolving industry.

HERE IS YOU FREE GIFT!

Network Configuration Templates

Exclusive Network Configuration Templates
Unlock our expert templates for everything from simple home setups to advanced cloud integrations, perfectly crafted to streamline and secure your network deployments.

Made in United States
Troutdale, OR
06/26/2024

20821669R00053